D0160290

Blue Genes

250 Rosedale Avenue

Blue Genes

A Memoir of Loss and Survival

CHRISTOPHER LUKAS

DOUBLEDAY

NEW YORK LONDON TORONTO

SYDNEY AUCKLAND

DOUBLEDAY

PUBLISHED BY DOUBLEDAY

Copyright © 2008 by Christopher Lukas

Published in the United States by Doubleday, an imprint of
The Doubleday Publishing Group, a division of Random
House, Inc., New York.
www.doubleday.com

DOUBLEDAY is a registered trademark and the DD colophon is
a trademark of Random House, Inc.

*Frontispiece photograph on p. ii from a family photo album:
White Plains, 1939. All photographs are courtesy of the author.*

LIBRARY OF CONGRESS CATALOGING-IN-PUBLICATION DATA

Lukas, Christopher.
Blue genes: a memoir of loss and survival / Christopher
Lukas. —1st ed.
p. cm.
1. Depressed persons—Biography. 2. Depression, Mental.
3. Manic-depressive illness—Anecdotes. I. Title.
RC537.L784 2008
616.85'270092—dc22
[B]
2008006648

ISBN 978-0-385-52520-6

PRINTED IN THE UNITED STATES OF AMERICA

1 3 5 7 9 10 8 6 4 2

FIRST EDITION

For Susan,

without whom I would not be living

'Round and 'round she goes . . .
Where she stops nobody knows.

—CARNIVAL PITCHMAN'S DITTY

Why are you so obsessed with death?

—J. ANTHONY TO HIS BROTHER,
CHRISTOPHER, SUMMER OF 1996

I'm not. I'm obsessed with living.

—CHRISTOPHER'S REPLY

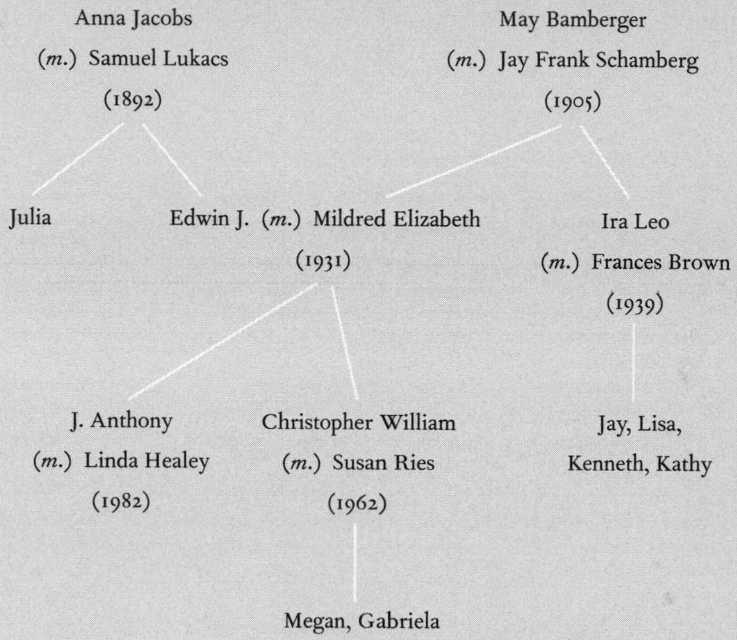

Anna Jacobs
(*m.*) Samuel Lukacs
(1892)

May Bamberger
(*m.*) Jay Frank Schamberg
(1905)

Julia

Edwin J. (*m.*) Mildred Elizabeth
(1931)

Ira Leo
(*m.*) Frances Brown
(1939)

J. Anthony
(*m.*) Linda Healey
(1982)

Christopher William
(*m.*) Susan Ries
(1962)

Jay, Lisa,
Kenneth, Kathy

Megan, Gabriela

Prologue

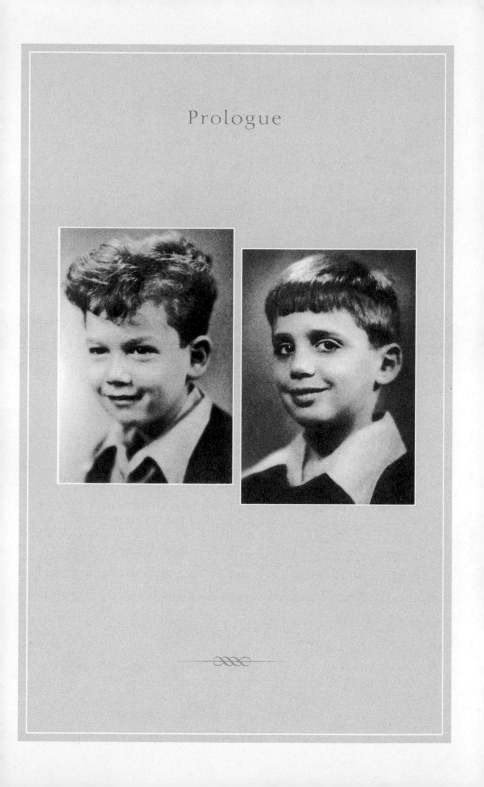

ON A LUSH MAY AFTERNOON IN 1940, my seven-year-old brother, Tony, and two of his pals from the second grade at the one-room schoolhouse down the road were playing one-o-cat baseball in our front yard. "Yard" is not quite accurate. The elegant, ten-room Revolutionary-era house in which my parents, my brother, and I lived for a few years in the late 1930s and early '40s was on seven acres of land. A small lake had been dug in the back of the house; rosebushes lined the south end of the property; and a small wooded area led, by a winding path, to a private school some miles away—a school to which my family hoped we would eventually go.

In short, we were upper-middle-class. Four white people, served by a "colored" staff of two, in prewar Westchester County, New York: privileged, select, unaware of the national, international, and personal doom that would soon descend upon us.

The stretch of greensward in front of our house was big enough for three young boys to debate the rules and practices of a game they had only recently learned, to ignore and place on the sidelines Tony's five-year-old brother—myself—and still leave room for batting, running, and catching.

The game was full of the sounds of boyhood play.

"You're out." "I'm not." "You didn't touch me." "I don't have to." "That was out by a mile."

I could clearly see that the game would be more enjoyable if they invited me to play. More pleasurable for them (another out-fielder) and more fun for me. But in Tony's view, I was too young to pitch, field, or bat. I was an outsider, not an outfielder. I was his awkward brother.

To me, none of that mattered. What I cared about was being *left out*. And, having asked politely several times to be included—and having been rudely denied—I decided to grab the means of production, the baseball bat, and see what transpired.

What happened not only says a lot about how Tony would approach the world in the next fifty-five years—as he sought and secured for himself jobs on major American newspapers, won two Pulitzer prizes, and wrote five important books—but also would establish the nature of our fractious relationship, a hands-off, hands-on kind of brotherhood that, in the end, was worlds away from the type of bond we wished to have. Fate got in the way.

While Tony and his friends debated a point of baseball arcana, I hid the bat behind my back, its knobby end showing clearly above my head.

Tony asked me to give it back.

No, more accurately, he demanded I give it back. By now, not sure of my position, as the three seven-year-olds began to advance on me, I grabbed that knobby end and began to spin the bat around my head.

"If you don't stop, I'll hit you," I declared, not exactly sure how I'd achieve that goal, but sure that giving in now would decide my fate for the rest of the afternoon.

The others stopped, but Tony continued toward me.

"Give me the bat, Kit."

"Not unless I can play."

"You're too young."

"I'm not. If you come any closer, I'll let go."

Tony was not frightened by my threat. In the years that followed, he would never be frightened by anyone's threats. He saw a frontal attack as the best course of action.

He advanced. I swung. How I aimed, I don't know, but the bat went straight to his temple and knocked him to the ground.

The other boys flew to their homes.

I ran into the house, sure that I had killed my brother.

Blue Genes

Chapter One

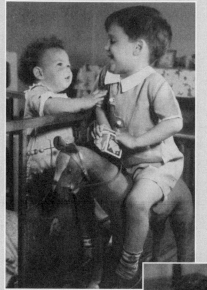

Big brother Tony with Kit, 1936 and 1938

SOME PEOPLE ARE DISTURBED MOST by events that are unexpected. For me, it has always been the half-awaited ones that carry the blow: the semiconscious fears that lurk behind closed eyes, the half-dropped pair of shoes, the what-ifs.

JUNE 5, 1997, 11:00 P.M.

Susan and I return home from a party. In an unusual show of activity, our answering machine has had eleven hang-ups and one message—from Linda, my sister-in-law.

"Christopher," she says, "can you call me, please."

Usually, no one calls me Christopher except strangers, but maybe Linda is echoing my brother, who sometimes calls me by my full name as a joke.

I make a mental note to call her tomorrow; it's too late tonight. I figure that she's probably planning a publication party for Tony, who has just finished his latest book, nine years in the writing.

The book before this one—*Common Ground*—resulted in his second Pulitzer Prize and dozens of other awards. One reporter called my brother "the best journalist of our generation." Another said he was "the patron saint of contemporary reporters." He has won numerous accolades for his reporting for the *New York Times*, has received honorary degrees for his deep analysis of crucial episodes in recent American history, and has been wined and dined by literati and academics alike. He is, in short, one of those remarkable men whose work received enormous respect and attention.

But Tony is not sure that the new book, a huge volume called *Big Trouble*, is up to his previous works. It's due out in a month or so, and we'll all have to wait.

While I'm at the closet, taking off my shoes, the phone rings again. Susan is near and she answers.

"Hello." A pause. "How?" Her voice is electric, alarmed. I recognize a disaster in the making.

I come around the corner of the closet, a shoe in one hand, the other still on my foot.

She looks at me, the phone to her ear, shaking her head, a look of terror on her face.

"What is it?" I ask, already feeling the pain begin.

"Tony killed himself," she says.

I scream and throw the undropped shoe at the far wall.

MOST BROTHERS HAVE SIBLING-RIVALRY PROBLEMS, interrupted by close bonding, but Tony and I always seemed to have great difficulty in finding common ground. The history of our family is partly responsible, a history full of self-destructive events.

In the wake of a family suicide, there is sorrow, guilt, despair—and anger. My reaction to my brother's death was no different; in fact, because of the difficult relationship we had had, it may have been worse.

During the first months after Tony's death, I viewed my life with him through the prism of anger. Why did he do this to me and to his family? If there had been good times in our years together, I didn't allow myself to remember them.

But gradually the truth seeped in: there was a whole store of other memories that I was hiding. I needed to make an effort to dredge up those experiences—the ones that had provided pleasure and comfort. To put a picture of our relationship in some kind of balance, if I could.

So, what would happen if I stopped thinking about all the rage I had for the way Tony had died and for the slights I had felt? What might occur if I recalled how much we had shared, what burdens we had lifted together, how we had supported each other? What then? I began writing about my family two weeks after my brother's death. At first, I could put down only a few thoughts about *him*, mostly about my anger and sorrow, but as the weeks and months went by, memories came—long-ago events that had been forgotten. Time passed; I would come back to the computer, put down new recollections. About us. About our relationship. I found memories of other family members, of the distant past, of things I thought had been obliterated forever. The mind is tricky: it brings back even the most distant feelings and events just when you think they have left you alone, left you in peace.

Today, more than a decade after Tony's death, I am still writing. But my idea of who my family and my brother were has changed over these years. The perception of who I was—and who I *am*—has also changed. So I keep writing. Trying to get it right.

A week after the suicide, when Susan, our daughters, Megan and Gabriela, and I attended a memorial gathering, Linda gave me a copy of *Big Trouble*, fresh off the presses. I turned the first few pages. In the dedication Tony had written, "To Christopher William Lukas. My brother, my friend."

That was an extraordinarily moving moment. I turned from the group around me and shielded my eyes, in tears. I had not had the slightest inkling Tony was dedicating the book to me. Nor could I have guessed that he would add "friend" to such a line. We were brothers—no doubt. But when all was said and done, were we really friends?

I decided I would start from there, from that emotional moment when it occurred to me that he really did care about me, that all the battles and absences and slights did not, in the end, seem to be as important as the fact that we were brothers—and friends. He had thought about me when he wrote that dedication. And perhaps he had thought about me even as he ended his own life.

CONFLATING THE PRESENT with the past is an old theme of philosophers. The idea of all chairs, said the philosopher William James, is present in the image of any particular chair. So any particular friend's essence is distilled by all the friends one has had.

And so it is with brothers. They are never what they appear to be to others, or even to oneself. Tony is a combination of past and present, of what he was and how I see him today.

But that is true of me as well. I am not merely the bald head in the mirror, the tired knees, and the naps in the afternoon. I am the sixteen-year-old with an enormous appetite, the twenty-two-year-old having his first real love affair, the thirty-three-year-old looking down at his first child.

Sister to sister, brother to brother, siblings can never be 100 percent fair about love and parental sharing and other sharp facets of the bright and painful lives they have together—even when much of that time is spent apart, even when they can communicate well and take the burdens of their relationship with good grace. I could not pretend that my brother and I were pals. Friends, perhaps, but not buddies.

Tony and I are brothers across the stroboscopic echoes of the past: dissolving across black interludes into the next image, and the next, and the next, until all vestige of pure vision is destroyed. All that is left is memory, and we know how faulty that can be. Who Tony was is forever blurred by who *I* was and how I remember who I thought Tony was. Yes, we are brothers in fact, in memory, and in wish, but he is dead, and I am alive—left to dwell on the questions, and to seek the answers.

There were questions of great importance to me: Would I, too, end up killing myself? Was the legacy of self-destruction I would discover in my family too great for me to survive? If so, when would the pendulum swing? And if it never did, why not? How could I—almost alone among my family—escape?

To answer these questions, I needed to go back and delve more deeply into my family and explore my relationship with Tony.

This is a story of two brothers in a *particular* family at a *particular* time in the history of that family. If the tale often appears to be as much about my parents and grandparents—and *my* emotions, *my* life, and *my* memories—as it is about my brother, it is because it is very much a story about relationships. The relationship my father had with my mother, the relationship of my mother to her parents. Mine with Tony, Tony's with those other people.

Beyond that, it is also a book about coming to terms with the suicide of a brother—an event I had written about previously when it happened to *other people*, but never before experienced for myself.

THE LETTERS, autobiographies, and other written notes have lain for decades in cubbyholes in an old rolltop desk that Susan and I bought on a trip to my uncle Ira's house near Philadelphia. The desk cost $40. At the time, I thought it was too much money to pay for an "old piece of furniture," but as usual Susan was right: you can always use a schoolmaster's rolltop.

Today, I love that desk. This is where the detritus of our lives lies. With nineteenth-century wisdom, its makers built it with myriad slots in which to stow important pieces of their complex lives. Into those compartments I have put the passports used for various family trips—their photographs attesting to the passage of time, change of hairstyles, even emotional states. I see Susan in early years, with downcast aspect, her hair tightly wrapped around her slender head, a strained smile on her face. I see her later, lovely brown tresses surrounding a confident, smiling countenance. And later still, the strands and flecks of gray shining in the sunlight of a photo I took myself. My own visages: young and shaven, a boy on the go; leather shirt from the 1960s; sideburns in the 1970s; finally, balding pate—"aging criminal on the go," the family said, jokingly.

Here in this desk went the birth certificates of our daughters, Megan and Gabriela, audiotapes of graduations and memorial services. Old keys. Legal documents. Currency from trips abroad. Broken pens. Broken promises.

It is through that desk, and from long-hidden events, that my memory is awakened. I take comfort that I can substantiate there the fact that Tony was not just a brother worth thinking about and arguing over on a personal basis but a complex, world-class character whose contributions to journalism and to his friends were valuable and whose death by his own hand is made all the more heartbreaking because it was not preordained.

Or was it?

What do I really know about the past? What do any of us know? Who were these characters? What led up to the deaths in my family? In truth, I was woefully ignorant—and, to be honest, fearful of finding out.

Chapter Two

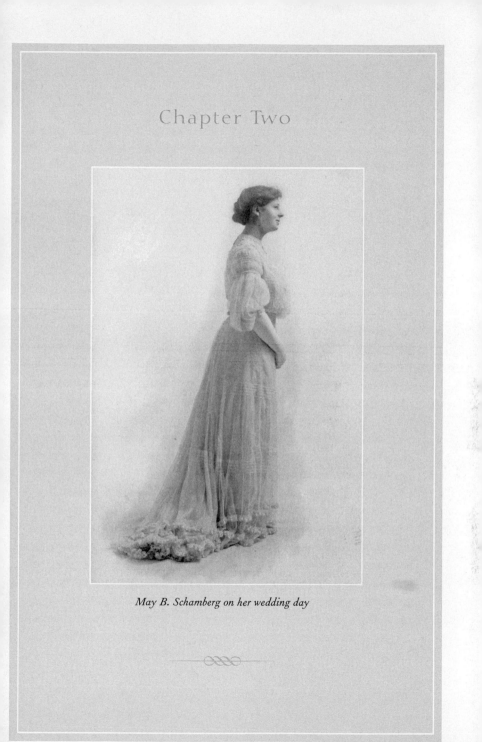

May B. Schamberg on her wedding day

MY PATERNAL GRANDFATHER, Samuel William Lukacs (or Lukacs Samu, as the Hungarians say), was a character to be reckoned with. He died crossing the Bowery in New York in 1927, well before I was born. I discovered this fact early one afternoon when Susan and I took Dad to the Nam Wah tea parlor in Chinatown. Nam Wah is the oldest dim sum restaurant in New York.

Leaving the tea parlor, where Dad had gagged on the food ("Don't they have orange juice and eggs, for Christ's sake?"), we started to cross the Bowery, that broad avenue that used to be known for its bums and drunkards. Suddenly Dad stopped in the middle and looked up and down the street. It was hot, he had eaten little, had had too much to drink the night before, and was in a foul mood, hungover. But at that moment, a strange, reflective, almost nostalgic look came over him.

"I think it was about here," he said.

"What?"

"The bus hit my father."

I had never heard about this accident. In fact, my father had never talked about his father, and while I found this strange—even baffling—having no guidelines about such matters, I never questioned him about his family past. Now Dad looked around, checked landmarks, nodded his head. We went on to catch a taxi so he could get uptown and have a "real breakfast."

Dad's younger sister, Aunt Judy (Julia), surprised Tony and

me when we were in our forties by relating how she had spent time at a Hearst paper in New York, writing advice to the lovelorn, when she was only nineteen. She had signed on to the paper in 1925 to do typing, but the woman who wrote the advice column was a friend of Mrs. Hearst's, and the two decided to take a world cruise. The editor told my aunt to write the column. Forget the fact that Judy was a naive young woman with no experience in the world of love or the lovelorn. Perhaps it explains her behavior in later life (she knew Tolstoy and Melville, but nothing about sex and love affairs). She agreed to take on the assignment.

Jump forward fifty years. Aunt Judy, horrified to hear how little I knew about my roots, takes to the typewriter again and writes me a long letter about the Lukas clan. Past—and present. It is very evocative.

Here is some of what I learned from her about the foreigners called Lukacs (the *c* was dropped when they emigrated to the United States).

Before World War I, Nagyvarad was the biggest city in eastern Hungary. That's where Samuel was born in 1865. Nagyvarad is in Transylvania—Dracula country—and was tossed back and forth between the Austro-Hungarian Empire and Romania for decades, depending on who won which war.

Like most Hungarian Jews, Samuel's family were Reform Jews, which meant occasional attendance at synagogue. At the turn of the century, Hungary had a fast-growing economy, and Jews were to be found in every aspect of business and commerce. In Budapest, every fourth person was a Jew.

Hungarian Jews were preeminent in math and fencing, but in Nagyvarad they were famous in other arenas as well. They taught, they discussed politics, they thought about the big picture. Samuel's family owned a café, so it was natural that he, even at a young age, joined his elders and sat in cafés, talking big talk. Aunt Judy said, "Father belonged in a café. He had all the qualities to make him popular there: he drank, he smoked, he laughed, he sang, he told endless stories with dramatic flair, he played cards; he teased the girls—young and old—and the girls, young and old, liked to flirt with him."

One of Samuel Lukacs's nephews was Paul Lukas, who became a famous actor, playing Shakespeare in Budapest when he was in his early twenties and later migrating to the United States. He, too, was popular with women, and in the 1920s barnstormed in small planes across the United States as he took work in both Hollywood and New York. Cousin Paul won an Academy Award for his portrayal of an anti-Nazi hero in Lillian Hellman's *Watch on the Rhine* and was on Broadway in numerous plays, including *Call Me Madam* with Ethel Merman. Tony and I used to go see him and have dinner afterward. There was some dissent about him in the family, since he had converted to Catholicism back in Hungary, but he was too talented to ignore. Besides, it was thrilling to have a famous person in our family.

At one of the dinners that Dad, Tony, and I shared with Paul and Daisy (Paul's alcoholic Hungarian wife), Dad asked him if he preferred movies or plays. Holding out his huge hands on either side of him in a dramatic pose, Paul said, "If a movie is here" (he clutched the putative film in one fist) "and a play comes along" (he opened the film hand to let the movie go, and grasped the "play" tightly in the other), "then I'd take the play." Even then, at the age of twelve, I remember thinking, he's putting on an act. I bet he'd take a film if it were more money.

Shortly after he turned twenty-two, Lukacs Samu met a young woman with whom he had a brief romance that broke off when the girl's parents discovered the dalliance. Which was why he precipitously left for the United States. Entering during the waning decades of the nineteenth century, he encountered Ellis Island but passed through successfully because he had some distant relatives here who could vouch for him. He remembered the experience, however, for later he took a job interpreting for some of the immigrants who aspired to live in the United States. He used the many languages he had picked up in that muddled part of Europe into which he had been born: Serbian, German, Romanian, Czech, French, and Yiddish, among them.

My Hungarian grandmother, Anna Jacobs, born in 1872, spoke German at home because that was the common language in her part of Hungary.

She had come to the States when she was three and learned how to be a seamstress from her mother, who was an expert at it and supported the family. Granny, as we called her, was diminutive and beautiful—so beautiful that in her late teens she took to modeling. She and her three sisters and brother lived with my great-grandmother in an apartment that opened onto the back of a Hungarian café. I think it was the one that Samuel Lukacs ran for a brief time. At any rate, Anna met him there when she was twenty, and they married in 1892.

I do know that my father thought Granny was too full of quiet resignation, too passive. He talked about that passivity often, saying he couldn't stand such "martyrdom." But he never told me what she was a martyr about. Was it Samuel's tantrums? Samuel's drinking? He didn't say.

But my grandfather did stand by her financially, even when times were tough for him.

By 1902, Samuel had moved with Granny to Jersey City, where my father was born, followed in four years by Aunt Judy. Samuel practiced the craft of watch repair (learned in his adolescence in Nagyvarad) but couldn't abide New Jersey.

Over the next fifteen years, the family moved many times: from New Jersey to Philadelphia; from Philly back to New York; then to Pittsburgh. Samuel's profession changed just as often. He gave up watchmaking for a hardware store, then traded that in to sell early models of the phonograph to the miners in the hills above the Allegheny River. My aunt remembers him striding around his study in Pittsburgh, comparing recordings of various arias—Caruso versus "unknown" tenors like Lazaro—and asking everyone in the family whom they preferred, so he could let the phonograph company know what it should support. Samuel thought Caruso was not the best; he didn't last long at that job, either.

"Every day started with excitement," wrote Aunt Judy. "He was an early riser. I heard him sing and whistle in the bathroom. I loved that. Then I had to be prepared for what would follow. My door would open and there would be some surprise. A funny face, a hand making signals, the growl of a monster. Before the day was over I would witness an endless variety of moods and antics. When he pounded the table at dinner, I didn't always know whether he was angry or having fun."

Some of this behavior can undoubtedly be chalked up to the "Magyar personality," the explosive temperament coming out of the tempestuous battles for survival in the old empire. But much was probably due to a particular set of character traits that I could sometimes find in my own father. He, too, whistled pretty tunes. He, too, broke into fiery anger at strange times. He, too, could be sarcastic—making jokes that were, or were not, funny.

My grandfather seemed totally unaware of the effects his erratic behavior had on Granny—or anyone else, for that matter. He was one of those theatrical human beings who was a whole world unto himself.

In Pittsburgh, Samuel continued to make enough money to

support the family with basics. Anna gave them luxuries with her sewing, including a piano for Aunt Judy, who couldn't play then and never did learn. Aunt Judy's first marriage, at nineteen, the one that took her away from the lovelorn column, was a disaster. "I married a Hungarian firecracker" is the way she put it. "And that's all I'm going to say about *that!*" I later found out he was twenty years her elder, an abusive man. When she married again in the 1970s, Dad helped get her divorce papers from Mexico.

Aunt Judy told me that Dad was popular with both girls and boys, who loved the way he had taught himself to play the mandolin and the accordion. Dad never mentioned his popularity. He spoke of the ugly, belching steel mills, and made it sound as if his family were poor. Aunt Judy swears they were not. Perhaps what colors how he remembered it were the vivid arguments he had with his father, especially about the outbreak of hostilities during World War I. Samuel believed the family should support the Hungarians, who were, of course, on the side of the Austrians, and therefore foes of the Americans. Dad was furious about this and argued in America's defense. When the "wrong side" won, Samuel pretended he'd been America's supporter all along. But they both shared dismay that the Allies had taken Nagyvarad from Hungary and given it to Romania. In some ways, it took the steam out of Samuel for the rest of his life.

Dad was also disappointed that his father wanted him to study dentistry ("to support the family"), a notion that Dad detested. He had his heart set on law and politics. However, to please—or at least pacify—his father, Dad entered the medical school of the University of Pittsburgh.

Dental studies were not as long or as arduous as those required for physicians, but the first semester was the same for both, mainly involving dissection. Dad told two stories about his dental school attendance, both of them quite amusing. Unfortunately, he told the same two stories over and over, until Tony and I knew them by heart, by which time they ceased to be interesting. One sticks most in my mind. It shows something about ingenuity, life in the 1920s in Pittsburgh, and my father's mind-set.

Dissection of the human body was done by teams of three students. My father picked two young men to do the work with him. Unfortunately, none of the three had the few bucks it took to purchase a dead body from the university, so Dad and his cohorts decided they could do what the dental school did: go to the coroner's office and get a body that was going to be buried in potter's field—the burying place for unclaimed bodies—and transport it to the lab themselves.

They looked in the paper and found the ideal body: a woman who had been dead only a few days and who, according to the paper, would be interred in a simple grave within twenty-four hours if no one claimed her. The three stooges approached the morgue and "claimed" Ella Morgan (the name found on the woman's identification, according to the paper). "A cousin," my father said. The official at the morgue laughed long and hard. "You're med students, huh?"

"How did you know?" they asked, chagrined.

"Come on, fellas, I'll show you."

Ella Morgan was black. None of the three applicants was. While Dad and his friends felt foolish, the pudgy official was delighted to have Ms. Morgan taken off his hands. He gave her to the students.

Ella weighed 250 pounds, which caused a number of problems. Outside waited the Model A Ford they had borrowed for the job. Piling Ella into the rumble seat was not easy, but they managed it. All three of them crowded into the front seat; no one wanted to sit with Ella. It began to snow, and the slippery, steep road up the hill to the university was too much for the Model A—especially with a dead body in the backseat. The vaunted ability of Mr. Ford's automobile to go up hills better in reverse didn't pay off, and the car skidded to the side of the road.

"We'll have to carry her," said my father.

And carry Ella they did, up many, many flights of stairs, stopping every so often to curse themselves for being smart alecks and cheap. Arriving, at last, at the lab's doors, they encountered another problem. They were locked. It was late. By now, tempers flaring and ingenuity at a low, they had only one choice. They broke a basement window, slid the body in, clambered in themselves, and carted Ms. Ella Morgan to an empty dissecting table.

As Dad put it: "In the morning, we could barely face one another, much less Ella."

Dad lasted that one year and then quit.

At the same time, Samuel and his family moved back to New York City, and Dad returned with them, joined by Lou Berko, a cousin with whom he had struck up an enthusiastic friendship in Pittsburgh. Together, they decided to go to a night course at Brooklyn Law School. It would take longer than going during the day, but they could have jobs during the day if they went at night. That would help them pay the tuition. Luckily, at that time, one didn't need a college degree to go to law school, so they both got in.

Lou and Dad pursued the law with intelligence and energy. To help support himself, Dad got a clerkship in the law office of one Fiorello La Guardia, a man who understood something about pulling oneself up by the bootstraps. He had done much the same as Samuel Lukacs, finding work at Ellis Island translating from Italian and the Slavic languages.

Dad liked clerking for La Guardia. The Little Flower (as he

was called by the press) believed in justice for the poor and in many of the qualities of democracy about which my father was now becoming passionate. Among Dad's duties for La Guardia was getting the famous stogies the mayor smoked. Dad tried one on a boring afternoon and was violently ill. La Guardia took no apparent notice, but on Dad's graduation from law school gave him a cigar box filled with those stogies. Dad was twenty-one years old.

This was not Dad's only escapade. On graduating from law school, and after taking the bar exam, he and his close Pittsburgh friend Lou decided to "see the country." Because neither had the money to travel in a comfortable manner, they decided to ride freight trains like hoboes. According to my aunt Judy, Dad took along a mandolin for entertainment. All went well for the first half of the journey. They traveled in empty freight cars, avoided the railroad police (the infamous "bulls"), and also managed to stay away from hobo encampments, where, according to legend, one could get killed for a few pennies.

It was the golden era of flappers, before the Depression sent America into a spiral of debt and despair. Jazz was played on the street corners and in the bars; pretty women danced in shimmering costumes. Lou and Dad could walk the streets unmolested, enjoying the exterior scenes and listening to the frantic music floating out from fancy joints. All that ended one night in July when they rode an empty car into the rail yards of Abilene, Texas. As they stretched their legs down to make the short jump to the ground, wondering where their next meal would come from—and their next shower—a couple of "bulls" materialized from behind a building.

"Gotcha!"

True to the town's frontier origins, the Abilene cops who captured Lou and Dad won a cash prize for every person they caught riding the rails, turning that person over to the local justice of the peace, who also was in charge of the jail. Scowling down from the bench, the judge sentenced them to ten days.

"You can't do that, Judge," said my father. "We're due back in New York for our appearances before the bar committee."

"Lawyers, huh!" said the justice of the peace. "Thirty days, then."

If some of this story is my aunt's hyperbole (Dad's short version was less exciting), so be it; enough is true to have cemented it in my memory all these years. As we heard it, the next thing that happened was that the judge's wife—who cooked meals for the few prisoners—took pity on the two young men and asked her husband to reduce the sentence. Calling them before him once again, he freed them, on one condition: they be out of town by nightfall.

Dad and Lou, sleeping gear and mandolin in hand, went down to the tracks. There was no freight train in sight, and a local hobo told them none was due through until after midnight. They had but one choice—to hide themselves behind the coal car in the flaps that stick out from the baggage car at the head of the line ("the blinds," they're called). So they rode the blinds to Denver, only to discover upon alighting—frightened and frigid—that coal dust had blackened them beyond recognition.

Neither Dad nor Aunt Judy relates how they got back to New York. Perhaps they had to call on their parents to rescue them. What *is* known is that they appeared in front of the bar ethics committee. Having passed their exams, they now simply had to tell the assembled men that there were no moral reasons why they should not be accepted into the New York bar. Dad told them about Abilene and jail and riding the rails. Looking down their rum-scarred noses at him, the committee members scolded him for his actions, asked him to think about what he had done, and let him leave the room thinking that they had serious doubts about his character.

As the doors closed behind him, raucous laughter spilled out from the committee room, and Dad knew that those peccadilloes were behind him. He would be admitted to the bar.

What always startled me about this story was not the minor infraction of the law but the independence of spirit shown by my father. To us—to Tony and me—he preached adherence not only to the law but to the *spirit* of the law. More than that: anytime that Tony or I broke away from the crowd, striking out with our own ideas or dreaming of great exploits, Dad would put us down. It was a clear case of "Do as I say, not as I do." Or was it a change in personality—something that happened to Dad as he got older: the fear that his adventuresome spirit might endanger his children, that we might prove to be *too* bold, *too* spirited, *too* independent, and he would lose us?

IF MY FATHER'S FAMILY—with its Hungarian bravura—proved to be too erratic, my mother's family, while appearing to be calm, cautious, mainstream, was a time bomb waiting to explode.

Our maternal grandmother, May Bamberger, was born in Brooklyn in 1884, fourteen years before that city became just another borough of Greater New York. Her parents were wealthy by any standard, but by German-Jewish standards well-off indeed, and May was treated royally. She went to a private school—the Packer Collegiate Institute—but not to college, having fallen, at nineteen, under the spell of a Philadelphia physician fifteen years her elder.

I have a photograph of her on her wedding day. Sweet and

beautiful, she wears a diaphanous gown that stretches to the floor and beyond, not with a train, but with frilly tassels and lace. A full bosom, full sleeves, hair coiffed up and away from her neck. Her nose is slightly upturned.

The doctor, Jay Frank Schamberg, had seven brothers and sisters; one of those siblings had ten children. I grow dizzy looking at the family tree. But May and Jay had only two children.

Early in her marriage to Dr. Schamberg, when the smallpox vaccination was introduced, May helped him spread the word that it was safe and effective. Later, when women she knew needed abortions, my grandmother often arranged for them, though her husband forbade her using the home to do so, since it would reflect on his professional respectability. And who can blame him? It would be another fifty years before abortions were legal in the United States. What amazed me is that my rule-bound, staid, puritanical grandmother was at one time at the center of a series of illegal operations.

She took other chances. At the beginning of World War II, May arranged for two English children to come over to the United States and gave their mother money to get started in a new land. She did the same for Anna, Ernst, and Marguerite Fuchs, Czech refugees who had fled to Paris when the Germans entered Prague, only to have to flee again when France was taken. Ernst Fuchs was immediately given important work in the war industry, and Marguerite Fuchs (his sister) took over the sewing department at the elite Elizabeth Arden shops. Only Anna—a college-educated woman—came down a step or two, rewarding our grandmother for the family's freedom by becoming her cook, and a caretaker for Tony and me. She would become much more than a caretaker: a guardian angel.

Some people said that May B. Schamberg (Missy, as we came to call her) looked just like Ethel Barrymore, the famous movie star, but prettier. She wore floor-length dressing gowns around her apartment and always paid for the best—whether in butter or beef or dry cleaning. I know about her early life only through a piece of barely disguised autobiographical writing of my mother's, a kind of "memoir à clef," which she wrote for a class in educational psychology she took in the 1930s. In that long essay, in which Mother used pseudonyms, she idealized Missy for her selflessness but felt there was something missing in her sense of self-worth. In fact, Missy was often depressed, rising in the middle of the night to cook or to play the piano, which she did with some degree of accuracy and no feeling whatsoever.

Because that psychology paper is so clearly an account of my mother's early life—as well as of her brother, Ira, her achievements and debacles, and the early years of my brother, Tony—I think of it as a long and powerful piece of correspondence: a letter, as it were, read by me after I ceased to be able to converse with her.

I first came upon it in 1971 after Missy's death. I was overjoyed to get some insight into the hidden facts of my mother's life, but in retrospect it has turned out to be more like a Trojan horse, replete with booby traps. Looking back, I wonder if it doesn't tell me *too* much about my mother's life and her relationships with those around her.

Mildred Elizabeth Schamberg was born on April 17, 1908. She came squawking into the world like many another child, although of course she was born at home, as were most children in those days. Dr. Jay had been cautious, however, and had a "specialist" present, rather than the usual family doctor. That obstetrician used forceps to bring Mother out. The umbilical cord was wrapped twice around her neck, but there was, the doctor asserted, no damage to the infant. Missy tried to nurse Mother, but the little girl didn't thrive, so a bottle was brought into play, and little Mildred

Elizabeth grew fast. Her baby book—a compendium of factoids about the newborn and her first six months—contained a section for gifts from relatives. I see listed there all those strange nineteenth-century names that clearly echo from my own childhood—names of the various great-aunts and great-uncles who peopled my grandmother's world. The gifts included one of those hollow metal dishes that allow oatmeal to stay warm by virtue of hot water poured into the interior. There was also a silver spoon from Tiffany, the date and time of birth inscribed upon it. I have them both, almost a hundred years later.

My mother had a very romantic notion about her parents. In the autobiography she describes them as a "Tennysonian husband and a Byronic lover." From other reports, ones I can trust, Dr. Schamberg was actually quite a distant husband and father. I have pictures of him, wearing a pince-nez and a vest. Many years later, my aunt Frances said he had been "a pill." She would tell the story of how, when asked if he was hungry, Jay would pull out his pocket watch. If the two hands met at noon, then he was hungry. Otherwise, not. Punctilious. Rigid. Victorian through and through.

As is the case with many German-Jewish families, there is little evidence that the Schambergs actually practiced any form of Judaism, except for the obligatory yearly Yom Kippur attendance. Still, Mother and her younger brother, Ira (born fourteen months after her), were often called "dirty Jews" at elementary school in Philadelphia. Ira had been born "weak and sickly, a little premature," but Mother reports that he stood up valorously for her if she was jeered at, and when they weren't fighting for attention from Missy and Dr. Schamberg, Mother and Ira were tight allies.

Apparently, the grown-up Schambergs were also disturbed by the cries of "dirty Jew" in the schoolyard because, shortly after Mother's tenth birthday, they surprised her by announcing that Dr. Schamberg had helped to organize a grammar and high school in the nearby suburb of Jenkintown. Soon, they moved there, and Elizabeth (her favorite name for herself, though some called her Betty and her brother occasionally called her Liza) spent an increasingly happy number of years at Oak Lane Country Day School.

Like many another rich family—and my mother's parents had plenty of money—the Schambergs often spent summers in Maine or other New England haunts. Often, Missy and Mother would go to Kennebunkport without Dr. Schamberg, who had to sweat it out in his office in Philadelphia.

When Mother was twelve, she went away to Camp Miramichi, one of those fake Indian hideaways where urban girls break up into different "tribes" and learn how to get along with one another. In her letters, which were often ten pages long, Mother was unlike the other camp kids I have known. She wrote with fine grammar and an even finer sense of purpose. To her father, in July 1920, she says that she hopes she hasn't made him angry for not writing sooner. Two weeks later she is begging her parents' pardon for having lied to a head counselor about taking some brown sugar from the kitchen back to her tent.

When Mother was thirteen, Francis Froelicher, who was in his late twenties, arrived on the scene as the new headmaster at Oak Lane. He took an immediate liking to her—to her quick sense of humor and to her appearance. Mother reciprocated. Over the next seven years what had started out as a childish crush became a dangerous liaison. In her mid-teens, Mother began to spend weekends as well as weekdays at the school. Froelicher was tutoring her in German and English and welcomed the teenager's avid study habits.

If this sounds like a budding Lolita–Humbert Humbert relationship, I fear it was far more prosaic, and far more dangerous. Froelicher was married—with three children—and knew better.

Mother was beautiful, smart, and precocious. She knew what she wanted and, before long, how to get it. I don't suggest that Mother was at fault here. There are too many stories of April–November affiliations in the newspapers and the psychology journals to blame an unstable teen for her desire to break out of a Victorian morality into an Edwardian one. Froelicher should have held his sexual desires at bay. He didn't; nor did he act ethically with regard to his job as Mother's headmaster. It was a terribly messy situation. I cannot take a higher moral plane than that: we all have made errors of judgment in our day. But I can say that what happened next was to have horrendous repercussions for decades to come.

Despite Froelicher's tutoring, and despite Mother's intellectual interests and achievements, she seems to have reached a little *too* high scholastically. On graduation from high school, she did not get into her first-choice college—Bryn Mawr—and went into a self-described funk. It was Froelicher who pulled her out of it and helped her get into then-second-ranked Goucher College, which she entered in 1924. Mother says she chose Goucher because Froelicher's father taught there. But it is more likely she went there because Froelicher himself recommended it. It was he, not Dr. Schamberg, who wrote her a long letter, telling her she was accepted. She was sixteen, Froelicher was thirty-two.

Goucher was good for Mother; she flourished there. I contacted the college—which is now coeducational and highly ranked—and managed to reach the secretary for the graduating class of 1928, who was still alive at ninety-seven. I asked whether she remembered my mother, and was astonished to find out that she did. "She was beautiful, and liked by all the upperclasswomen," the secretary said.

Goucher's alumni office sent me the class yearbook.

I thought I had become accustomed to seeing new photographs of my mother, but the bright-eyed, beaming, stunningly beautiful young woman of twenty who looks out from these pages was a startling revelation. In one photo, she is standing with six other students. They are dressed in the style of the day: fur coats, bobbed hair, bowl-shaped cloche hats. Mother, the tallest, has her coat thrown back to show her tight-fitting dress. A scarf circles her neck, and her head is not covered.

Compared with the other students, she was spectacular.

At Goucher, Mother's best friend, Frances Berwanger, became a companion with whom she could express loving feelings. They exchanged poetry, visited each other's homes, and spent summers together. There were rumors that Frances and my mother had a sexual relationship—rumors I heard from my aunt and uncle—but in her autobiographical essay, Mother says no.

At the age of twenty, she was about to graduate, looking forward to "real life." While she had corresponded with Francis Froelicher during her four years away and, when at home, had often run to tell him of her activities, their relationship had remained somewhat distant. Now, she thought, things would change. But as she contemplated acting upon what had only been a dream before, Mother realized that what she wanted was impossible. I don't say "wrong." There is no hint in her writing that Mother felt a moral reluctance. But she knew full well that Froelicher had a wife and that Dr. Jay would find the relationship between his young daughter and this man anathema.

So, before her last semester of college, she broke off with Froelicher, vowing that she would not see him again. It was of necessity a hard decision.

To her mother:

Of course yesterday was ghastly for me in every way: it means
the breaking of a contact which I suppose no one can understand,
but which has been practically my chief source of inspiration for

the past six years. If I behaved badly I hope you'll attribute it to the emotional strain of the whole business. Must go to bed—I hope really to get some sleep tonight.

Reading this letter for the first time—and digging into what the autobiography revealed about this period of my mother's young life—I was shaken. The rumors of this illicit relationship, overheard in bits and pieces at my aunt and uncle's house, paled in comparison to the actuality. My own love life at a comparable age had been rocky. I knew what it was like to give up a precious relationship. But nothing really prepared me for what Froelicher and Mother had undergone. Shaped not only by the mores of the 1920s but by my own late fifties sense of right and wrong, I could both identify with my mother and feel trepidation at what it meant for her future—and for mine. Hindsight, in this case, gave me little clarity, little comfort, little optimism.

AFTER GRADUATION, Mother wanted to get away. From Francis, from her parents, from the whole mess. Picking up on a parental promise, she planned to go abroad for a year, taking Frances Berwanger with her. But that was not to be. Her friend was only a sophomore, and Frances's mother didn't think the trip was a good idea, perhaps afraid of the lesbianism that had been rumored.

With the idea of a trip with Frances stillborn, Mother nevertheless made a brilliant year out of it. Off she went to London, where she enrolled in the Royal Academy of Dramatic Art (RADA), the only American allowed into that hallowed institution that year. It was 1928, she was twenty years old. Stars of the British stage had been trained at RADA for decades. It was a difficult leap for an American to make, and yet, from all reports, my mother did remarkably well. Perhaps her warmth and sense of adventure outweighed self-doubts that any emotionally precocious person might have—and my mother had them in spades. Or perhaps being away from her family gave her freedom to be outgoing.

I have read the reports from her instructors at RADA. They praise her elocution and diction and her sense of stage presence. "The teacher told someone that I have one of the most beautiful Shakespearean voices she has ever heard," Mother wrote to Missy. "Imaginative and sensitive," wrote another teacher. They cannot promise that she will succeed as an actress, but perhaps . . .

Outside of class, self-doubts *do* assert themselves. Her inability to concentrate on any one thing at a time alternates with anxiety, which in turn alternates with depression. What will become a diagnosable illness in a few years is more than an annoyance, though less than debilitating. Still, midyear, she writes Missy that she is "sick at heart," a euphemism for depressed. Then she beats a hasty retreat in a follow-up letter:

> *I had allowed myself to give way to what was a very temporary mood, and by doing so caused you real concern. The problems of which I spoke are really minor.*

We can't know whether Mother believed this or whether she was so used to hiding the truth from others that this was yet one more chicanery.

Missy had a brother, Morton Bamberger, who had gone to fight on the side of the British in World War I by enlisting in the Canadian Air Force. Enchanted by the English way of life, Morton turned Anglophile and anti-Semitic in one fell swoop: he changed his name to Morgan Blair and settled down in Sussex to raise racehorses. The great flu epidemic of the 1920s killed him, but not before Elizabeth had met him and he had introduced her to a sixty-seven-year-old polymath, Edward Heron-Allen—who had, among other achievements, translated *The Rubaiyat of Omar Khayyám* into English from the original Arabic. He tried to seduce Mother. Failing in that, he gave her an autographed copy of the book, which I have on my shelves. To Froelicher she wrote an inquiry: Did he think she should have acquiesced? Was it better to be loved by an older or a younger man? This disingenuous query was answered at once by Froelicher. Perhaps she should wait, he suggests.

It doesn't take any reading between the lines to know what Francis wanted her to wait *for*.

In retrospect, I am startled by how little reaction I had when I first got all this information of sexual and emotional transactions. This, for me, was more like opening a lost history book and discovering facts and aspirations, desires and denials that were unknown to mankind and are now revealed.

Mother's letters reflect not only on *her* life and emotions but on her mother's. Missy was not happy. She, too, showed signs of depression and anxiety. Approaching the age of forty-four, she decided to embark on psychoanalysis, and at one point Elizabeth wrote from England: "No news from you in several days leads me to believe that you are plunged into the very depths of psychoanalytic gloom."

There is no reply from Missy.

After studies, Mother toured France and England, returning to the United States in 1929. Clearly, she had learned a great deal, because she was asked to join the repertory troupe of the director and actress Eva Le Gallienne, whose company was making artistic headlines. What roles she played, and where she toured, are not recorded, but at one point she must have found herself near Francis Froelicher, because they picked up where they had left off a year earlier.

The news of the relationship finally reached Dr. Schamberg. Perhaps it had been rumored for years, and now, finally, someone actually told my grandfather. One did not need to be a rigid Victorian to object to one's twenty-one-year-old daughter getting involved with a married man with three children.

In the few remaining years before his death, this liaison—now out in the open—was a subject Dr. Schamberg never spoke about to his wife or anyone else in the family. My mother says that he couldn't bear the fact that his daughter had been "so lacking in standards" and that his friend and protégé, Francis Froelicher, could behave in such a disloyal fashion. It was "an unbearable disillusionment."

Dismayed by the agony she had caused her father, Elizabeth once again promised to stop seeing Froelicher. And Francis promised not to write her. As a teenager, Mother had been a camper in far-off Maine. That summer she decided to go to the Tripp Lake Camp, as far away from Francis as possible, to be drama counselor. Tripp Lake was the kind of place where wealthy Jewish thirteen-, fourteen-, and fifteen-year-olds spent four or five weeks in canvas tents and wore middy blouses with lanyards and baggy blue shorts. Rising early in the chilly mornings, they stood around the flagpole singing songs. Then they peeled off to shoot arrows at straw targets, paddle canoes on the big lake, and compete for parts in weekly dramatic productions. Mother adored the camp's owner, Caroline Lavenson—a friend of the family—who reciprocated the feelings.

Despite promises made on all sides, Francis and Elizabeth kept up their correspondence:

There was a letter waiting for me here, and an eight page one yesterday. His resolve not to write evidently proved impossible to keep. I've answered both letters. Of course, I miss him, but there is much compensation here. I'm finding pleasure in this work.

As the year wore on, the pair broke promises right and left. Exactly what transpired between them has been lost to burned letters and unspoken confidences, as well as whatever actions could not—or would not—be spoken about. My mother confided some things to Missy—who, it turns out, was not only undergoing psychoanalysis but having an affair of her own—and they supported each other in these secrets.

Then there was silence: nothing in my file of letters for the next year, not between Missy and my mother, nor between Francis and my mother. I suspect that my grandmother dispensed with those letters that bore dangerous secrets; or Mother did. It was a "thrilling, but painful" year is all my mother would say in her memoir.

On his side, Froelicher was clearly fighting his own moral and practical battles. He made what must have been a hard decision. He told Elizabeth that he would look for a better, higher-paying job and, when he had money put aside, he would leave his wife and marry her.

But as the country entered *its* Depression, Mother entered into her own increasingly intense periods of pressure and desperation. She knew that Missy would "stand by her no matter what she did," but she was equally sure "that she might just as well kill her father as to do this thing."

"This thing," of course, was to run off with Francis. And other factors weighed in. There was a large sum of money waiting for her in her grandmother's trust fund; if she married Francis, she knew she would be disinherited.

Chapter Three

Elizabeth and Edwin J. Lukas, 1930 or 1931

ENTER EDWIN JAY LUKAS. After graduating, Dad had begun the practice of criminal and civil law. In a few years he would join the firm of Sapinsley and Santangelo. Later, when Santangelo became a judge, it was Sapinsley and Lukas.

Alvin Sapinsley handled the civil cases that brought in money. Dad took care of the less remunerative civil cases and—increasingly—the criminal ones. In later years, he spoke only of the latter. And more and more he took on cases that brought in little money—cases of indigents and the underclasses.

Somewhere in the bottom of the pile of letters through which I have been rummaging I came across *this* snippet, from a woman whose name was unfamiliar to me. It was written to Missy in 1932:

> *A short time ago, I read of a lawyer, Edwin Lukas, offering his services free of fee as a defense counsel for a Negro couple whose case interested him (as it did me) and who, through utter ignorance had gotten themselves into a lot of trouble. What a splendid act of true charity and proof that ethics have not yet gone entirely out of the world.*

One of my father's friends was an actress named Anna Kostant (later, after she married a real estate magnate, she was Anna Bing). Anna knew my mother through Le Gallienne and thought she would be a good match with my father.

Dad and Mother met and immediately saw something within each other that struck a strong chord. They were both energetic, both endowed with good looks, but there was more. For my mother, my father was a way of keeping her from being tempted by Froelicher—at least for now. For Dad, there was something endlessly enticing about this sparkling actress from an upper-class family. Mother had a clear sense of Dad and approved of his goals and activities.

He was a self-made man who, while not yet successful, had been working since he was fourteen, helping to support his family since his father's death, alone supporting his mother and sister. He had had no time for an education beyond the one which would win his bread and butter for him. He was sensitive, intelligent, keen, passionate, though uninformed on most of the cultural matters which are important to me, and six years my senior.

There are a couple of misalignments in this assessment. For one thing, though far from "cultured" in the sense that Mother meant, Dad was an extremely well-read man. It might be that he thought orchestra conductors were show-offs, and, to be sure, his idea of classical music was pretty much limited to Tchaikovsky's *Romeo and Juliet* overture; his opinion of abstract art was that "a monkey could do that just as well." But if you wanted to talk Samuel Butler or Dostoyevsky, he was your equal. And if you ventured further, into the realms of social philosophy, ethics, government, and certain arenas of psychology, Dad could beat you at your game as fast as Uncle Ira would whip me at chess.

He was of his period and time. His politics were to the left of center, though nowhere as far left as those of some of his neighbors who formed a Communist cell. He believed in civil liberties and civil rights—in other words, what the Constitution said. When he was in his fifties, he led a strong organizational push for civil rights, even filing an amicus brief for his employer, the American Jewish Committee, in *Brown v. Board of Education* at the Supreme Court.

He *was* elegant. My wife says his hands were two of the most beautiful she has ever seen. I am pleased to resemble him somewhat. There is a photo of Dad at his desk in the Fred F. French Building on Fifth Avenue when he is in his mid-thirties. Compare it with me at the same age and you can hardly tell us apart: thin, balding, severe.

Dad was also an elegant speaker and writer. Mainly self-taught, he had learned how to create phrases for papers and speeches that went beyond mere rhetoric. His journal articles and speeches are models of engagement and clarity. He was an extemporaneous speaker of note. Whether at a graduation ceremony or an assemblage of colleagues, Dad could rouse, persuade, encourage, and damn the audience with what appeared to be minimum effort. Suddenly, before they knew it, people were with him in whatever cause he was espousing.

SOON AFTER DAD AND MY MOTHER MET, Missy's mother, Reba Bamberger, was introduced to my father and was charmed. Shortly afterward—much too shortly, to my mind—Edwin asked Elizabeth to marry him. She told him about Francis, and he asked her again. For three months he asked her, and one day she said yes. My mother wrote that "it seemed the only possible solution for everybody." (Froelicher was clearly still in her heart and mind.)

On February 4, 1931, at the ages of twenty-two and twenty-nine, respectively, Elizabeth Schamberg and Edwin J. Lukas became engaged. They went riding together in the Philadelphia and

New York parks, each sitting erect on a good-looking horse. They went dancing and on cruises.

IT WAS NOT A GOOD ERA for the country. President Hoover had failed to rescue the banks and the population from desperate times. Unemployment was at 25 percent. Hoovervilles, encampments for the dispossessed, had sprung up all over the United States. Average salaries plummeted. Food prices sank. Milk was fourteen cents a quart; bread, nine cents a loaf; steak, forty-two cents a pound. And even then, at those low prices, millions of people couldn't afford basic commodities. Hoover nonetheless steadfastly insisted that while people must not suffer from hunger and cold, caring for them must be primarily a local and voluntary responsibility. But there were no safety nets, and the country sank deeper and deeper into the Depression. Despite such nationwide desperation, Mrs. Bamberger had done well. A cousin had urged her to sell stocks while they were still high, and she had kept her money in safety during the terrible crisis of October 1929. Now she moved into the Langdon Hotel just off fashionable Fifth Avenue and Fifty-sixth Street in New York City, gave her legal affairs to my father to handle, and started dispensing sufficient sums of cash to Missy and to the engaged couple to allow them to forget that Hoover and the country were failing. Soon, Franklin Delano Roosevelt would ride in on his white horse to rescue the rest of the population.

Like Mrs. Bamberger, Dr. Jay and Missy took to Dad immediately. What was not to like? He had begun his legal career smartly and was already being talked about in New York circles (Dr. Schamberg did his due diligence with friends in the city).

My mother, in turn, fell for Dad's mother, Anna, and my aunt Judy, both of whom reciprocated. She described them as "impecunious," and her attitude was always a little condescending, but that was in part the attitude of all the Schambergs. Still, there was no doubting the couple's rightness for each other, no "class" distinctions to be made. Dad, whatever his roots, was clearly a man for all seasons.

The marriage might have gone ahead without a hitch except that Elizabeth began at once to have second thoughts. She was not *really* sure that she could ever love Dad as much as she had Froelicher.

For his part, Francis tried to do the right thing. He knew now that my father-to-be existed and was engaged to his darling Elizabeth. He wrote the following letter to Missy:

Feb. 1931.

Dear Mrs. Schamberg:

It was generous and kind of you to leave a message for me here in Philadelphia. I must try to believe that only my absence and silence will serve Elizabeth. I like to think of her as our Elizabeth, because I am sure that no one else can come to know her quite so well or love her quite so much. Reading and re-reading your letter has been a great comfort for me. It tells me that one person, the nearest to Elizabeth, has a pretty clear understanding of my situation. I know the natural effect of time. I cannot want her to forget or to put me entirely apart from her life; I do want her to be completely happy. But my life, in fact, belongs to Elizabeth.

Francis.

Missy was an endless romantic. That she was also a meddler did not come home to me until I read the following from my mother. Missy had apparently not only been in touch with Francis Froelicher but told my mother about his letter.

Dearest Mother:

There is one thing which you could do for me, if it doesn't appear to you an unnatural or unpleasant task. I think Francis would appreciate it more than you can imagine, if you'd write him a note saying that you feel we've done unquestionably the wisest thing or however you want to put it. And saying also what you've so often said to me about his influences on my life. He has a real affection for you and I think if he felt your continued goodwill and friendship it would help him immeasurably to bear something which now seems intolerable to him. Could you do that? Don't let him feel that you think it was my decision alone in the case of our separation because it wasn't, or that it was yours or anyone else's influence on me. F. and I made it alone. I am not writing to Francis or hearing from him.

Calm and determined as her note to Missy sounds and feels, in the same envelope is a smaller letter in which she told her mother that "according to your instructions, I have gone to see Bernard Glueck," my grandmother's analyst.

It has never been a good idea for family members to share the same therapist. Since Glueck and his wife were personal friends of the Schambergs, it was an even worse idea. The good doctor saw my mother for fifteen minutes, squeezing her in between other appointments. According to her, he felt that "the marriage was okay" and that it should "take place as planned." Mother says she had asked whether it wasn't too soon "as I've so barely recovered from the other thing." But Glueck says he thought a delay would "gain nothing."

In what can only be considered a second bad judgment, the psychiatrist urged my mother to turn down a part in a play that Le Gallienne had offered because it would go on the road in the spring. Mother says she is "divided" in her feelings. Is it the tug between Francis and my father that divides her? Or between the play and staying with Dad? She doesn't say.

For my part, "living" these events many years after they occurred, I feel as if there's a bad genie at work. Someone is pulling strings from outside the frame. Given Mother's oncoming mental disorder, the Froelicher affair could only have ended badly for all concerned. Nevertheless, Mother's creative outlet in acting was a strong life force for her. What would have happened if Glueck had practiced in today's world? Would he have still thought that a marriage and children were the most appropriate "escape" from a romantic tie to Francis, and would marriage to my father—so soon after breaking up with Froelicher—have been a remedy for depression? I doubt it, and it makes me angry that he interfered so strongly and so wrongly.

The wedding was small, took place at the Langdon Hotel, and resulted in a $10,000 bearer's bond passing from Reba Bamberger to the Lukases. It would be well used on a house five years later. For the next year, there were no letters between the newlyweds. I consider this a good sign. It means they were *with* each other, staying close to each other in their apartment in New York and planning their future together. But Mother said that all was not well.

The next thing that went terribly wrong was that Dad was told Francis and Mother continued to be in touch.

The person who did this was Caroline Lavenson, the woman who ran Tripp Lake Camp. Looking back, I cannot imagine why Caroline felt she needed to warn Dad about Froelicher. At this point, there is *no* evidence that Elizabeth and Francis were continuing the romance. Mother was emotionally beaten down, but she seems to have given herself over to Dad in every way that I can discern.

I don't know whether Dr. Schamberg and my grandmother found out about this indiscretion on Caroline Lavenson's part, but I do know it would have profound repercussions on my parents' relationship until the very end.

And certainly it did not help the young couple's relationship that, a few weeks later, Missy gave a huge box of letters and other material to my mother—labeled "The Private Papers of Elizabeth"—and told her to go through them to sort which she wanted to keep and which to get rid of. The letters from the clandestine year may have been thrown out at this time. Mother wrote to Dad, "I have spent the evening with ghosts, and though there is no fear in me there is much thought and speculation."

Speculation, indeed! How could Dad know what was going on in the mind of his beloved? How could he know what she was doing? Or thinking?

What *is* clear is that the two of them now began a dialogue where a certain doubt had been injected into the relationship, and that doubt remained—permanently.

Take the end of that year, for instance. It was almost New Year's Eve, and, upset and perturbed, Mother had gone to Philadelphia to spend Christmas with her parents. Dad was not included. While there, Mother went to visit the Lavensons and from there phoned Dad. What transpired in the call is not known, but its *character* can be judged from the letter she sent him that evening:

My darling:

You break my heart with such talk as we have just had. I feel that I can have been only the most cruel and stupid of people to have allowed you to suffer like this. Certainly you must know, despite your protests to the contrary, that much, much has been done in this past year towards the rebuilding of my life. I have often

said, and more often thought, that your understanding has been
unbelievably self-effacing, and perhaps I've relied on that too
much, much more than was fair to you. I want so much to make
you happy, and yet I seem only to achieve the contrary. Any hu-
man relationship is a difficult thing to work out, and ours, having
started out with certain added obstacles, needs more skill and pa-
tience and love than most. I'm spending these three days at home
and hope to be rested enough in body and spirit to present a saner
outlook on your return. I think my curious inexplicable feeling
and behavior of the last weeks has been sheer weariness. Yes, I
know I'm stubborn, but at least it's put to one good use: I stub-
bornly persist in loving you.

The recognition that she hoped to present a "saner" outlook gives
some evidence that by now my mother was beginning to feel the
more intense pulls that would soon blossom into full-scale bipolar
disorder—that complex mental illness, sometimes called manic
depression, in which waves of a depressed state alternate with
some form of mania, the ups and downs coming without much
warning, and sometimes getting deeper and higher and deeper
and higher, without relief. A person who is bipolar can become
catatonic—unable or unwilling to get out of bed or do the usual
chores. Alternately, a manic-depressive can be ferociously active,
sleeping very little, exhibiting a great deal of energy, sporting
many creative ideas, spending money wildly, or madly performing
sexual activity. Unfortunately, the science of psychology was too
much in its infancy to be much help to my mother. Today, many
medications are available to tame the bipolar beast.

At the end of 1932, Mother and my father were in need of the
kind of help they were never to get.

Having gone to upstate New York with Missy, for a short visit to some friends, Mother wrote a letter to try to tell Dad what she needed from him, and what he could expect from her. She was, she said, beginning to discover in him some of the same worries and mental jumping jacks that pursued her from time to time.

At this time, sick of "taking money from Mr. A. to give to Mr. B.," Dad was planning to give up the civil cases that were bringing some money into the law partnership. It would be some years before he left the firm altogether, but he was already worried about his career, which he didn't think allowed him to make a great enough contribution to society. He was also deeply worried about money. He didn't want to depend on the Schambergs' wealth to sustain his own family. He wanted to be independent.

But my mother saw his financial doubts as only part of the problem:

> *Edwin, you really worry me badly at times. I seem powerless to dispel your deep gloom. I think there is an alternative to letting this money thing possess your mind and soul. There is much beyond the ugly pettinesses of our existence which is waiting for us to explore and which remains full of reward to the curious seeker.*

By the time she wrote this letter, Mother had been pregnant with my brother for five months. Later, as winter bore down on her for her first delivery of a child, she felt compelled to write Dad again.

It was a long epistle, written from a distance (again, she was with Missy), and clearly some troubled exchanges had preceded it. In it, Mother expressed dismay that Dad refused to believe that she loved him. "You are tormented by doubt of me." My father would never lose that doubt. And my mother would, more and more, be sure that it was a failing in *herself*.

J. ANTHONY LUKAS WAS BORN ON APRIL 25, 1933, two years after my parents' wedding.

Shortly after Tony's birth, my grandfather's heart gave cause for alarm. He was sent off to Stanford, New York, where it was cooler than Philadelphia and where Missy could take care of him. Mother and "the infant" traveled there, too. While Tony played in the sun with his grandfather, Mother watched them both and wondered if she could ever feel the joy that other mothers felt for their children—and for their fathers and husbands. As she wrote in her journal:

> She watched the aging man and the growing baby lying together on the lawn and wondered whether they would ever really know each other and whether Tony could give her father the love she wanted to and could not give.

None of which is what she wrote to Dad. To him, she said:

> Your Tony boy has been angelic and he is the admired darling of the household. Grandma has him in bed with her every morning and he coos and gurgles vociferously in response to her rapturous adoration. But we both miss you, my darling, and he will coo and I will be glad when you are with us again.

Soon, Dad and Mother began looking for a proper place to settle down. In the country. For a while, they rented places in Westchester for the summer. But Mother was certain the air and foliage would be better for everyone if they could find a permanent place outside New York. Dad didn't want to commute, but Mother won the debate, and they found a year-by-year rental in New Rochelle, not too far by train from New York.

Dad was stewing and worrying about his choice of career: whether he should do more for the outcasts of society and less for the rich and famous. He also worried about his wife. God knows he loved her, but he found that she was indecisive about household matters, overspending when it was not called for, and then panicking. He worried—Caroline Lavenson's warnings continually echoing in his ear—whether she was also indecisive about him, whether Froelicher was going to be a persistent, silent stalker in their relationship.

Mother had her worries, too. One potential house rental had a wet bar in the basement. Dad wanted to take the place, and in a letter to Missy, Mother wrote, "I only hope I won't have to seek refuge in your arms from the curse of a drunken husband."

In the fall of 1933, Mother decided to get a graduate degree in education so she could teach. She studied such newfangled psychological materials as Rorschach tests. Tony was left in the hands of Mary (whom he came to call Baba), a young black woman who also labored with cooking and other chores. In her autobiography, Mother says she used Mary's presence as an excuse to stay away from the house and from Tony, with whom she began to feel she was "inadequate."

It was during this course of study that she wrote in the autobiography:

Gradually a state of anxiety took hold of her and, though she continued to run to school each day and go through motions, she felt that she had ceased to dictate her own conduct.

Mother lost her appetite and her ability to handle social situations. She would panic, her hands perspiring, her heart beating faster and faster. She felt she needed to learn from Missy how to deal with "the household," perplexing problems such as the best cuts of meat, what to do about laundry soaps, the maid's time off, the linen closet. By now, however, Dr. Schamberg was seriously ill, and Missy was needed elsewhere.

Finally, Missy could spare some time. Mother met her at the train station, in tears. She had been unable to order dinner because she couldn't decide on a leg of lamb or a roast beef. The indecision left her distraught.

That night, unable to really express to her mother the total load of anxiety, but somewhat more secure in the knowledge that her mother had her competent hands on the household now, she took a large overdose of medicine.

Looking back, with all the power of modern psychological knowledge, it would be easy to make a diagnosis. What Mother had was bipolar disorder. In the 1930s, there was no one who made that clear diagnosis.

Today, too, we know about postpartum depression, with its hormonal component and its propensity to spring up where there isn't enough social support for the mother. Postpartum depression is said to affect from 15 to 20 percent of women in the United States. In our family, where there is a genetic predisposition toward mood disorders, it's not surprising that our mother suffered from that disorder, with its insomnia, sadness, guilt, hopelessness, and thoughts of suicide. Unfortunately, at the time, few knew about *that* disorder, either.

More troublesome still is how strong an effect depression in the mother can have on infants. Mother exhibited a wish that her child disappear not only so that her own "incompetence" would not be a burden but also so that Tony would not be a burden on *her*.

The result was disastrous. As psychologist Dr. Sandy Zeskind has said:

> The mother may reach to take the baby's hand, but if the baby pulls his hand away, so does the mother. It's almost like she gives up on the interaction. Over time the missteps add up. The baby displays sadness and irritability and starts to take on the mother's depressed affect.

In short, depression can be seen as a "communicable disease," transferred through a mother's communication to her baby. The consequences for Tony would be lifelong. The brilliant English psychologist D. W. Winnicott reassured parents that it was impossible to be perfect. But it was—he assured them—okay to be a "good enough mother." From the distance of over six decades and as someone who lived through the life and death of my mother, I can say that she was *not* good enough.

Missy and Dad debated what to do. Psychoanalysis? Hospitalization? They once again decided to rely on Dr. Glueck, who had a sanitarium called Stony Lodge, near Ossining, New York.

When Mother entered Stony Lodge in February 1934, the procedure for massive depression and attempted suicide was twofold: insulin shock therapy (massive injections of insulin resulting in convulsions and coma) and careful observation. Insulin shock as a treatment for schizophrenics and others with severe affective disorders had been discovered in Europe only a few years earlier. In fact, 1933, the year of my brother's birth, was the first time it was tried in the United States. It seemed to work, though the convulsions it caused were not controllable. Later, in 1937, researchers discovered that electroconvulsive therapy (ECT) was better than insulin shock, causing most patients with severe depression to feel better. Because the convulsions produced mild amnesia (and fewer broken bones than insulin therapy), no memory of the traumatic treatment remained to hinder patient cooperation. After some years of banishment because of its appearance of torture, ECT is back in fashion: much better controlled, and used only for the most desperately depressed patients. Mother would have been a good candidate.

For now, however, there were talks with the doctors, some insulin shock therapy, a ban on sharp objects, and a lack of freedom to wander around the grounds. Shortly after arriving, Mother had tried to pierce her jugular vein with a paper knife, so for now she was never left alone.

Nonetheless, she wrote to Dad almost every day—at first in pencil (no pens permitted), then in ink. The notes began with a few tentative sentences expressing her intense guilt at having disappointed him with her suicidal acts. Later she added promises "to be good." In her autobiography, which she continued writing after getting out of Stony Lodge, she made perfectly clear that she felt she had *betrayed* Dad in thought, that she had continued to yearn for Francis Froelicher long after marrying my father. Now, in her letters, she strove to make up for those treacherous thoughts.

March 15, 1934
Dearest:
We will move to town; we will do everything that can make up one iota to you for the pain I've caused you. You are henceforward my guide in all these things.

March 19
Dearest:
We shall both need great patience but I hope to be really worthy of you soon. Please stop talking about becoming worthy of me. You can do a good job by concentrating on Tony for the pres-

*ent, in any spare moment you may have. I am going to get well
for you. If you can be as remarkable a father as you are a husband, Tony will be a very remarkable fella.*

But if Tony was going to be remarkable, he was also going to
suffer from the fact that my mother could not relate to him.

When they brought Tony to see her she wept bitterly, only because she felt nothing for it. When Edwin came to tell her that
her father had died she could not weep. She felt nothing and was
agonized that she could not feel. She had ceased to care for the
first time in her life what people felt about her, and faced the
horrible fact that she herself was devoid of feeling for most
of these people.

By the first week in April, Mother was writing letters about
normal activities, urging Dad to find a place in New York City so
he could be near his work. At the end, she returned to the hidden
theme in both of their minds: "Please, dear boy, remember and believe that you are *the only man* whom I love. Go to sleep knowing
it and wake up knowing it, too."

On April 11, she was talking about how much freedom they
were giving her at Stony Lodge, and then, "It's all very odd, this
thing called the human being. I don't know yet what's caused all
this but I guess I'm destined to find out."

Her final letter from the sanitarium, written on the day before
her birthday:

*April 16, 1934
Edwin, Darling—
    The knowledge that we love each other and have years of joy
and sorrow, struggle and achievement ahead of us together makes*

*me overlook the bad weather. Both of us have much to learn and
I know we can do it . . . as always I thank the powers that be for
you.*

Ever yours.

And so Mother came home.

It is hard to remember—all these years later—that I am writing here not about two mature human beings, in their middle age. Not the stern and distant father I remember when I was growing up. These are young, struggling people. Mother was twenty-six at this point; Dad was thirty-two. I can only imagine the horror my father would have felt at having a suicidal twenty-six-year-old return to our home, and how fragile a time period it would be for *any* young mother, much less one with a mental illness.

Within two months of her return home, Mother was again pregnant. It was me. I was born on March 6, 1935. Given what had happened after my brother's birth—the postpartum depression, the attempted suicide—why did my parents decide to have another child? Perhaps it was an accident; perhaps they didn't know the cause and effect between pregnancy and some depressions; or perhaps it was an example of hope triumphing over reality.

Whichever, it was a difficult pregnancy, and a difficult birth. There is a very testy letter from my mother to Dad in January 1935, berating him for not paying enough attention to what the obstetrician had determined was a medical abnormality in her, as her due date approached. Whether this was anemia or some unknown disorder is not clear, but she says that my father was not concerned enough. Perhaps Dad thought it was an overdramatic reaction on her part. Or maybe—and I have done this myself—it was one of those male denials that anything could go wrong, that there might be another disastrous turn of events.

As it turns out, I was born cyanotic, what's called "blue baby syndrome"—either a genetic glitch or too much deoxygenated blood being taken into the lungs. Lips and tongue turn blue. Dad gave a pint or two of blood to bring me up to par. After that, I thrived, putting on weight as if I were eating seven meals a day.

OVER THE FIREPLACE in my present home is a large portrait of my brother and myself, painted when we still lived in the old colonial house in White Plains. I am four, and Tony is six, though the artist—good as she was—has put a much older face on my brother. I wear green corduroys with a bib and straps and a red long-sleeved shirt. Tony is in a saturated royal blue shirt and dark red corduroys. The straps of his trousers are crossed, shortened, in deference to the fact that he was beginning to shoot up. Mother wanted him to have room to grow into them.

I remember posing for that painting. We stood in front of a French door that looked out on the back of the house. I was bored and didn't want to stand with my brother's arm around me, staring out at the recreation room, when it was warm and pleasant outside and frogs and other playthings beckoned. But I did as I was told, because I was a "good boy."

When outsiders look at the painting, it is clear to them that Tony and I are well fed. The color of our eyes isn't quite accurate—mine were actually lighter than his—but they are good eyes, with a clear view of our world. What is most striking about the painting are the strong differences between us. I am a curly blond, Tony's hair is straight and black. His complexion is umber in tone, with almost a greenish tint, like our mother's; mine is light, like Dad's. His lips are thin and pale, mine almost like a woman's and bright red. Allowing for the artist's choice of color and line and her attempt to make us look part of the same family of colors and tones, it is almost impossible not to see that we are far apart in terms of looks, but we were also far apart in terms of temperament.

The ovum is fertilized. Immediately, it splits into two, then four, then eight, carrying with it into the multiplicity of cells copies of new genes, made up of the DNA of mother and father, but in a different combination from before. Each of us inherits from the same parents, but in permutations that dictate some of what we will be. Nothing can be said to be solely responsible for our future looks, behaviors, actions, feelings—but this random splitting and distribution are a big part of it.

Many of the differences between Tony and myself were inborn. The physical ones are easy to see. But I think much of our emotional and psychological differences were also due to the hybrid tossing of genetic matter.

Still, not all character traits are from our genes. Nature and nurture work together, and though my brother was always darker in color and spirit than I, there is surely more to it than his inborn temperament. As all of us grow from infant to adult, we learn to tell our own stories, our personal worldview. Sometimes, we construct good stories. If we're unlucky, we build unpleasant ones. Luck, skill, fate—all play their roles in who we become and how we face the world. The remarkable thing is how long Tony survived.

If you regard my brother in that painting closely, I believe you can see clear through to his soul. In his eyes, you can see the dark, brooding boy and man that I came to know—the Tony who shows in his photos a serious intent, his lower lip pushed out just a little, his elegant fingers clasped in front of him. Tony of the "raccoon eyes," rimmed with dark shadows. A wounded look sometimes crosses his face—as if he has been stabbed or punched in the solar plexus. I recognize the same look from my father and my grandmother: a wounded bear in the forest or a deer about to be run down by a car could not have stared with more hurt and, often, more anger.

I HAVE READ MOTHER'S LETTERS to Dad shortly after my birth. She had taken Tony and me up to Marblehead, Massachusetts, where Missy had a summer rental. While Dad slogged along in the sweating city, practicing the kind of law he would later abandon, Mother enjoyed cool sea breezes, unlimited space, and coddling by her mother. In one of those letters, she says, "Kit bubbles with delight. He is pure joy." Missy wrote: "Kit is Master Sunshine as usual; easing his way into everyone's heart."

"Master Sunshine!" While Tony was what—"Master Gloom"? That was the difference people saw between us. The big painting in my living room already describes that disparity. But if the psychologist was correct—and Tony's depression stemmed from Mother's depression—then what went right with me? Was Mother a beaming, communicative person with me, whereas with Tony she had been a gloomy woman who could not take her son into her life? If so, Master Sunshine I remained—to the outside viewer. Inside was a different story.

Meanwhile, while everyone cooed over me, they ignored the huge blue elephant lying about our household. No one wanted to express either hope or pessimism for the future.

As promised, my parents moved back to New York, into an apartment in a brownstone on Ninety-second Street on the East Side. There, the first year of my life was spent in relative ease. I was a fat little baby. There is a photograph of me sitting in a tiny sleigh—the equivalent of a stroller—dressed for winter, a fur throw on my legs, pudgy cheeks puffed out against the cold. My family finds it hilarious.

Then, in an about-face and a burst of enthusiasm for Dad's growing law career, and for the money that he was making, and with a boost from the "manic" phase of our mother's illness, my parents splurged and bought seven acres in White Plains, with a large white eighteenth-century house. It was here that Tony and I spent the next four and a half years.

This was the dream house that every American couple wants. Like all such dreams, it came at a cost. Since it was the Depression, the property cost only about $10,000, but that was already two and a half times the average cost of a house in those days. (The Dow Jones Industrial Average was only at 134, and the annual income of a wage earner was $1,800.)

Mother decided the house needed a lot of work. They put another $5,000 into fixing it up with appurtenances like large, curved windows in the dining room and living room, a screened-in porch for summer guests, and a screened-in bedroom for Tony. I have seen some of the correspondence between Dad and the contractor during the months it took to do the work: endless problems with the sump pump, with the supporting walls, with the special glass they'd ordered for the windows. Dad threatened to stop all payments. The contractor threatened to stop all work.

Eventually, it was finished, and I remember the result as being quite remarkable. Aside from the huge rooms, the gorgeous furnishings, and the ample space to play indoors, outside there were all sorts of delights. Huge apple and pear trees sheltered the ten-room house from the summer sun. They would have borne rich fruit if they'd been fertilized, but that fruit became rotten at once, attracting hundreds of bees. In the front, where the sun could reach them, roses were planted. Mason jars of poison were attached to green stakes to attract and kill Japanese beetles. I watched the jars fill up, then scurried to tell my mother.

Up a gravel driveway, which ran parallel to the front of the house and up a slight incline, there was a two-car garage. A beautiful cherry tree decorated the bottom of a hill that stretched back a hundred feet, with a rock garden full of fragrant herbs. I recall that I learned my ABCs on a little stone seat there, chanting them in time-honored fashion until I had committed them to memory many months before my peers would do so. Mother believed in preschool education long before *Sesame Street* arrived on the scene.

On one side, woods bordered the property. On the other, a picket fence ran along Rosedale Avenue. Missy contributed to the funds for the house. Sometimes she contributed trimmings that were neither expected nor wanted. My parents came back from one trip shortly before we moved in to discover that she had commissioned a small lake to be dug in the back two acres; steam shovels were driving across newly laid crocuses.

"It's a present," said my grandmother. Of course, whether they wanted it or not, my parents had to take it. There was no going back.

Decades later, I went to visit the house. Normally, adults think that the places they lived as children have shrunk in size, or at least diminished in grandeur and beauty. For me, it was the opposite. Even though the house itself was a little run-down (two of its black shutters were askew; paint was peeling on the upper dormers; the grounds needed maintenance), it was *bigger* than I remembered it. I looked for additions since I lived there, sixty-four years ago, to account for the size, but there were none. It was just plain large—with many rooms, hallways, porches. The old, rotting apple tree had been pulled down; a pool had been installed where the rose garden used to bloom. Over half of the acreage had been sold off to other property owners. But the garage and rock garden remained. And so did the lake, which was also larger than I recalled. It filled over an acre of land. I walked down the road to West Street, turned left, and stood looking at what used to be the one-room schoolhouse where I attended kindergarten and first grade. Miss Honeywell, a rotund woman in her forties, taught eight grades, each with no more than five or six students. Still, we must have been a handful. On the front of the building, now a comfortable home painted a robust barn-red color, a plaque announced that the building was constructed in 1884. I remembered the potbellied stove that kept us warm in the winter. I remembered everything, and my eyes filled with tears.

I DON'T THINK I UNDERSTOOD that my family was very well-off. At the age of five, I had no such perspective. I didn't know that families existed all over the country with no one to drive the car or cook the meals or put their little ones to bed. Though almost every upper-middle-class family had at least one person to help with the chores, ours had two. And this was during the Depression.

When I went away to school, it wasn't Groton or Exeter, it was coeducational and "progressive": more chinos and blue jeans than flannel slacks; more outdoor activities and chores than perks. We were forbidden to have expensive items in our bare-bones rooms. Egalitarian in the extreme, it was a place where we were meant to ignore differences. No, it was more than that: we weren't supposed to know that money was a factor in people's lives.

I grew up believing that a happy life did not require having a lot of money, that work was beneficial for one's soul as well as for society, and that equality between the sexes was a given—and constructive to boot.

Nevertheless, for much of my young life, I was coddled, protected by Missy's largesse.

IN HADES, there is a river called Lethe. For those who drink from those waters, the past becomes obliterated. It's not clear to me who in the big white house at 250 Rosedale Avenue actually drank, but they all *appeared* to be oblivious to the immediate past: nothing bad had happened.

It was a grand illusion.

All continued to think they were living a golden life. On weekends, visitors sat with the family in capacious Adirondack chairs on the side lawn, sipping iced tea. A formal dining room was the scene of parties—not just for the grown-ups but for the children as well. I remember my fifth birthday. A number of neighborhood children were invited to an Italian feast. We had fake noses (Pinocchio had recently been in my reading material) and ate spaghetti.

Willows grew quickly in the moist soil at the edge of the lake. Even the algae that persisted in the lake were of a quality such as to make friends, relatives, and even ourselves shimmer with delight at the sheer beauty.

Fall was the most devastatingly beautiful there ever was. Spring, the most pleasurable.

Our nanny was warm and generous and devoted to us. She was married to a man who lived elsewhere. Where he was or when she found time to see him was unclear, for she took care of us and did housework and cooked a good deal of the time. Tony had named her Baba, an infant's attempt to merge "Mama" with "Mary." She was kind, attentive, and aware of everything that went on in the house. I have a photograph of her in our garden in White Plains. She sits, primly dressed, quite small, quite young, in a large rocking chair. On one side, his arm leaning on the chair, stands Tony in a striped T-shirt. He is three years old. I, clutching the chair to steady myself, stand on the other side. Both of us wear shorts. My curly hair needs cutting. An impish grin is on my face, and Baba looks with great love upon the scene. In her lap—a book and a ball, some of the paraphernalia of her work.

When I was four—still, by all reports, a sunshiny, precocious child—photos show me smiling all the time, but a little too chubby kneed and precious for my taste. My famous actor cousin, Paul, offered to take me to Hollywood, where I would become—he said—the male Shirley Temple. My father, bless his soul, demurred.

All the photos and accounts tell the same story: I was fair and curly haired and ran everywhere after Mother. Tony was deep and dark and troubled, his sallow coloration and furrowed brows signaling troubled inner thoughts. When he was six or seven, my parents sent him to a psychiatrist. Perhaps they saw Mother's earlier abandonment of him as the cause of his sadness; perhaps he had bad dreams. Perhaps there were more pressing problems. No one ever informed me.

Later, as adolescents, when we saw Joe Btfsplk in *Li'l Abner* cartoons, we felt that Tony, like Joe, was always under a cloud.

Was he the wearer of blue genes, inherited from Mother and her ancestors; or was he reacting to her suicide attempt just after his birth? Or both? Or was he simply unlucky? Whichever, Tony always exhibited a sense of sadness.

There was another person in attendance at the Rosedale Avenue home: Proctor. This tall, sturdy African-American served as occasional chauffeur, as well as man of all trades, fixing the lawn mower, the sump pump, the kitchen sink. He lived above the garage and became, by default, an educator to Tony. By *default*, because in many ways Dad was not able to act as a paterfamilias. His concerns about Mother, his concerns about his career, created a father present in body but not necessarily in mind.

So it was Proctor who taught Tony to ride a bicycle, how to bat a ball, how to garden, weed, harvest. In later writings, it was Proctor whom Tony credited for his devout interest in professional baseball.

There must have been times when the entire family—all four of us—was together during these early years, but I have only one strong recollection of such an occasion. It overshadows all the others.

At the age of five, Tony had already learned the rudiments of swimming. Since I was two years younger, I was tentative about even wading into the lake. The bottom was muddy, and I feared snakes or snapping turtles, so I stayed on the small sandy ledge about six feet from shore, calf deep at most.

One Saturday, however, as Mother in her bathing suit watched from the bank, I was encouraged to wade out farther—where the water was deep enough to swim. I went slowly into the unknown—afraid to dog-paddle but also afraid to take my feet off the muddy bottom, worried I might sink. I was on tiptoe when I felt a little wavelet and suddenly thought I was going to go over the top of my toes and drown.

Panicked, I cried for help.

From a few yards away, Tony struck out for me, as did Mother, diving in from the bank. Then I saw that my father, dressed in a fine summer suit, was stripping his jacket off. He, too, dove into the water.

I quickly realized I *wasn't* drowning. Still afloat, I shouted, "I'm fine!" and started dog-paddling toward shore.

Everyone was relieved that I was safe. But Dad was furious that I had ruined his suit. "Don't cry wolf unless you *mean* it," he shouted. "Look what you've done!"

I still try not to cry wolf, and I try to believe that Dad loved me. I am not totally successful at either.

ROSEDALE AVENUE WAS WHERE OCCASIONAL LAPSES foretold distant events.

I remember sitting one spring with my mother, in the rock garden, listening to the birds and watching the shadows of a great elm tree play against the front of the house. Mother was quiet, too quiet. I glimpsed in her beautiful face some distant thoughts that were not for me or for repetition.

I remember Dad coming home at night, tired and cranky, usually too late to come up and say good night, though I strove to stay awake long enough for him to do so.

Missy used to visit several times a month, taking the slow train up from New York City and remaining several days.

There are some photographs of her when she was in her twenties. Tall, regal, with prematurely silver hair. There is a picture of *her* grandmother that I've seen, too. It was at the New-York Historical Society some years back. Titled "Mrs. Bamberger Comes to America," it portrays a well-dressed woman, floating, fully clothed, in the ocean while clinging to a piece of flotsam. Behind her a vessel appears to be swiftly sinking, its four masts barely protruding above the murky water. The painting was done in the nineteenth century. It's based on a true incident that involved my great-great-grandmother. On Mrs. Bamberger's face there is no sign of panic, no sense that she is in danger. She will make it to shore and will go on with her life.

I hold this image in my mind, knowing that some people come face-to-face with disaster, then, letting go of the debris, turn their backs on the past and survive. Most of us are treading water, even though we don't know it. What we do next is the crucial thing.

I remember Missy walking across the grass at 250 Rosedale Avenue. It was six in the morning, and she was in her nightgown; I can almost *feel* the dew on the lawn as it softly rinses her bare feet.

The sun crept up over the woods that bordered our property. Birch, oak, and maple trees, shining in that lustrous morning light which I remember well, beckoned to those of us who were awake. As soon as I was able to walk, I became an early riser, and I liked to put my elbows on the windowsill in my room and watch the sunrise, the squirrels on the trees, the change of seasons in the rose garden that bordered the house. But this memory of Missy has always been confused with a photograph of another white-haired woman, also in a nightgown, also barefoot, walking across the grounds of an old-age home in the Midwest. This shot appeared in *Collier's* magazine as part of a story on forgotten people. In remembering the picture, I always think of the place as an insane asylum, not an old-age home. And I always think that it is Missy walking there, not some anonymous old lady, lost in her crazy thoughts. I know I really did watch her in those early mornings, rounding the corner of the rose garden, her head down, her long prematurely white hair falling over her shoulders, dreamily experiencing the coming of day. I always feel the event not as Missy says she felt it—a lovely oneness with nature—but with a premonition of terrible things to come.

In the late 1930s Dad made a decision to get out of courtrooms. He didn't actually do it until late 1940, and there are several versions about how this happened. His friend Robert Lindner—the psychoanalyst who made a stir as the author of *Rebel Without a Cause* and *The Fifty-Minute Hour*—told me that Dad had been asked by a big importer-exporter client to go to Veracruz, Mexico, in the fall of 1940. Apparently Mexican authorities were holding up permission for a freighter to leave port for Japan.

Dad found out why and phoned the owners.

"Your father was drunk when he called from Veracruz," Lindner told me in 1955. "He had discovered that the owners of the ship had a cargo of scrap metal they were sending to Japan. By this time, such shipments were embargoed. The United States knew the Japanese were going to use scrap to make planes to fight China, or ourselves. Your father hated being used that way. So he told the owners to shove it."

"He was drunk?"

"Yes," Lindner said. "He'd had half a bottle of tequila."

This was the first I'd heard of any such behavior on Dad's part. It was very dramatic. The resulting unemployment and attendant anxiety would haunt the family for years to come.

MEANWHILE, TONY AND I BECAME CLOSE COMPANIONS, not just brothers. Much of the time, we enjoyed each other's company. Other times, it was a sibling relationship, like any other: testing and torn.

There were two bedrooms for us. I had the interior one, and Tony slept on a large porch with storm windows that sat on top of a screened-in porch below it. Tony's room was big enough to serve as our playroom, and there are photographs of us, playing with blocks, then toy soldiers, and finally a bunch of marionettes. One of my favorite photographs, a large 8×10 that has been laminated to a wood block, shows the two of us dressed in kneesocks, matching long-sleeved argyle sweaters, *Blue Boy* shirt collars, and ties, playing with our soldiers on top of a huge set of blocks in Tony's sleeping porch. We seem to be having a good time of it.

In my room, a bed was pushed up against one wall, and a toy chest against the other. I could look out over the rose or rock garden, but the room was dark enough so I could take naps in the afternoon. My favorite stuffed animal, a penguin, nestled next to me on the bed, and I remember the texture of the tan blanket that lay underneath my bedspread: it felt soft and furry and was probably very much akin to the "blankie" that most young children cling to for security.

Tony and I went to bed at the same time—a practical matter. It was easier to treat us as having the same needs than to feed or read to us at different times, with different stories. I know this annoyed Tony and occasioned many a "Go away" when I tried to catch up with him or accompany him as he broke away from set routines or explored the woods with his pals. But at meals, we were together.

And at bedtime as well. While we both lay awaiting sleep, we would have a conversation between the two rooms. Sometimes this was plans for playing cops and robbers the next day, or finger painting, or exploring the ferns around the back side of the lake. At one birthday we acquired some toy bows and arrows. When a gaggle of older boys passed our driveway one afternoon, we fired the suction-tipped arrows at them. Naturally, the light pieces of wood fell harmlessly to the road, far short of their target. The boys went away; when they returned, they came with hunting bows and steel-tipped arrows and scared the shit out of us.

We played well together in the earliest days, though occasionally our jocund recreation became antagonistic. Tony might hound me about a particular piece of verbal stupidity, some word that I could not get my mouth around, such as "spaghetti" or "radiator" (which came out "pisketti" and "elevator"). Once or twice he jumped out at me from a dark closet, scaring me into tears. He also locked me in the same closet a couple of times, even though he knew that I was terrified of closed-in places, so much so that I had nightmares for years of being buried alive. In those dreams, I had somehow become entombed in a coffin; dirt was being piled on top of me. I could shout, but I couldn't be heard. I would wake in a panic.

As far as I can tell, none of Tony's pranks were pathological or truly hostile. They were the normal give-and-take of siblings. Had they persisted into adolescence, that would have been a different matter.

One fall, a fire broke out of control when Proctor and Dad were burning leaves. Tony ran to them with a garden hose, but the picket fence was beginning to be lapped by the flames. I sat on the front steps, my arm in a giant cast, a broken arm from a fall off a skittish Arabian mare. I asked Mother why no one had called the fire department. A lightbulb went on in her head, and the local crew arrived quickly. I was rewarded with a little metal medallion for my inspiration. Tony was jealous.

Tony had another use for the garden hose under less frightening circumstances. The water was cold, summer days were hot, I was younger than he. So, as a joke, or as punishment for some of my "misdeeds," he would wait for me to come around the corner of the house, and then spray me with the hose. I was not amused, but later I learned to turn the tables on him.

There was another summer activity that was a lot more fun. A half mile down Rosedale, where it meets Mamaroneck Avenue, was a tiny grocery store. No one in our family shopped there, but once we reached a certain age, Tony and I were allowed to walk there in the summer for ice cream cones. I favored chocolate; Tony, vanilla. The cones, costing five cents each, were fully packed, so we had enough for the walk home. The game we played was how long each could make the ice cream last, who could say, as the other finished his dripping cone, "I've still got *mine*."

I loved sitting in the front seat of our station wagon when Dad or Proctor or Mother drove to the station or the farmers' market or to pick up Tony from his violin lessons. I played with the window handle, turning it this way and that as if I were steering. It was an elegant vehicle, a Ford, with wooden frame and slats (what the Brits call an estate wagon), polished until it gleamed.

When we weren't using the car, it often sat right in front of the house, as if it might be needed at a moment's notice, left in first gear to keep it from sliding.

One day, when I was about five, I got into the driver's seat. I knew how it went: you get in, you close the door, you push the little button on the dashboard, and the car goes. So I got in, I closed the door, and I pushed the little button. And it went. Apparently the brake wasn't on.

My feet didn't have a chance in hell of reaching the floor, and I doubt I would have known what to do if they did. At first I was delighted—no panic. Then *lots* of panic. Then screaming, as the car chugged up the little incline and—luckily—stalled. There was a moment of fear that it might go backward, but the gear held. I slid from the seat to the driveway: guilty, frightened, relieved. I remember no consequences for my naughty act, except having one more guilty escapade to add to my list—a list that would keep growing as I got older.

Dad and Mother went to Mexico one spring for a brief vacation. We were left to our own devices—under Baba's and Proctor's guidance, of course. When our parents returned, carrying chairs from Guadalajara and other memorabilia, we were aware that there was more and more tension between them. One night, waking from a frightening dream, I tramped down the long hallway to knock on their door. Then I opened it. I started toward Mother, but Dad intervened. He was furious.

"Get back to bed!"

He chased me down the hall, and as I scooted into my room, crying with fear and shock, I hollered for Mother.

"Get into bed," he screamed again. I wanted to stop to take off my slippers, which I had carefully put on as I prepared to go for comfort to my mother's arms. Dad would have none of it. Into bed I went, slippers and all. The door slammed on my room, and then on their room.

I was terrified of my father. And I hated him.

Crying, hurt, uncertain about my safety, I pulled the covers up over me, pretending that I was in a boat on the ocean, safe, watertight, far from harm. Tony, in the next room, never awoke.

In some of the psychotherapy I underwent in later years, it was suggested to me that Dad's fury had to do with my intervention in a sexual event—the "primal scene" about which Freud writes. I dutifully listened to this interpretation, but I reject it. I think that *my* motivation may have been Oedipal (*What is going on behind that closed door?*), but the scene I saw in my parents' bedroom was not a happy one, much less sexual. Mother sat in her bed, a scowl on her face, Dad in his. I remember how much Dad liked his sleep and hated to be interrupted. But what I recognize now is the tension between them, and Dad's fear that Mother might be getting manic or depressed again, that she might be in touch with Francis. And Mother must have had her own terrors: What would happen to her? What would happen to all of them?

THE MOST IMPORTANT PART of our early life in White Plains was undoubtedly the little dramas Tony and I staged on the window seat in the dining room. This even had a curtain that could be pulled to close off the entire window seat from the rest of the house. There, at the ages of six and four, respectively, my brother and I began to play out our feelings, making up plays to express ourselves through mime or rudimentary dialogue. This was at the urging of Mother, the actress and budding educational psychologist.

Tony was the writer, of course, but Mother was the impresario, and the audience as well. She applauded, encouraged, critiqued, and supported our little theater company. Only years later did I realize that this seed of theatricality, implanted in me at that early age, became a life force. It was a result, I later realized, not of our mother's desire to have us express ourselves but of her inability to ask us directly how we felt about things—to *connect* with us. The plays were the only *real* contact our mother had with us. At meals, at bedtime, at all the normal points of communication between mother and child, we were Baba's children.

When Aunt Judy came out to the country, she would type up some of the plays that Tony wrote, and we might perform them in the big playroom in front of a larger audience—of three or four. Naturally, the writer took the hero's roles; I played villains. I played Hitler to Tony's Roosevelt, and later I would play Stalin in *Prussia Under Pressure*, Tony's four-minute playlet about the German retreat from Moscow.

In adulthood, I often looked back at those experiences as key to understanding not only my love of the make-believe of theater but the depth of my need for applause. These were the times that Mother spent concentrated, in-depth "quality" moments with us. This playacting on the dining-room banquette stands out as a time of pure pleasure and excitement. Mother was, at those times, in love with us, and we were in love with her. I speak for Tony because I think I can claim without doubt that he shared my pleasure in our mother's joy and intensity.

Chapter Four

Reading time, 1937

IF MOTHER COULD LAUGH AND APPLAUD at our little plays, the rest of the time she was more and more in the throes of unwelcome feelings. Sometimes up, sometimes way down, always in doubt about the strength of her husband's belief in her. Always in doubt as to whether she could give him what he needed. She felt that Dad would not express his love for her as she imagined other husbands or lovers did: with wooing and sweet words. She believed he doubted her trustworthiness. She doubted her own trustworthiness. They both doubted the relationship.

Perhaps Mother was simply realizing that her needs as a woman were not to be met by this rational, twentieth-century man. Perhaps he was realizing that his needs as a man could never be totally satisfied. But that would leave out all the other history and pathology. Mother ends one letter, "I can't get past the idea that underneath all the formalities which we scrupulously observe, neither of us has a very good idea of what the other is thinking or feeling."

I know you are weary and overburdened with worry and I don't like to be an added one. I've tried to do my part in minimizing my demands on your strength and energy. I know I am childish and immature—call it what you will—but I need a little spoiling, a little petting, a little manifestation of the feeling which compelled you to say not so many years ago, "I want you under any circumstances."

Maybe you don't know that when one has been wooed and won under such circumstances you don't stay won just out of inertia. You start to watch the years slipping along and you see your children leaving babyhood and you know that soon you will have left your real youth behind, and you don't want to leave it without some deep and abiding experiences which belong to you alone, by nature and by right.

I'm sorry to have had to say so much. When we discuss these things orally we can't seem to do it without anger and harsh words, so I'm putting mine on paper in all sincerity and without any intent to hurt you or—as you think—to be unfair. This is one last attempt *[emphasis mine] to put my viewpoint before you, with the hope that you can see what I mean. I don't think I'm unnatural or different from other women in my hungers and needs.*

Perhaps that's the trouble. You thought once that I was an angel. Though you've modified your idea in most respects, I think you still hoped that I was free of some of the "peculiar ties" of my sex. It's too bad, I can't live up to that hope.

You are such a grand person and I love you so much; I could love you more if you gave me the chance. I respect and admire you and I would like our marriage to be something we could both look forward to and back upon with pleasure and joy as well as responsibility and pride.

With much, much love. Elizabeth.

I have read this over and over, hoping to change the words, hoping to change her mind. I cry now as I have not cried before. As I look at the total sweep of their lives, I feel my mother and father are doomed.

They just don't realize that nothing can possibly match their fantasies of what life is supposed to bring. For Dad—and I know this from his lifelong behavior—women were never smart enough, beautiful enough, or comforting enough to calm his soul. He needed to be stroked and fed and soothed. For Mother, the genetic blow she had been dealt created a perpetual state of anxiety or depression. Bipolar people have a heightened sexuality. Mother wanted a romantic male to woo her constantly. I want to shout at them, "Get real!"

IN THE SUMMER OF 1941, Tony was offered the opportunity to go to Treetops, a camp in upstate New York. He accepted gleefully, and for the first time I was left totally alone with Mother. By now, Dad had left the law firm. He took off each morning to meet with those who might help him find another career, something more suited to his wishes to be of public service.

Being alone with Mother meant piano lessons, peanut butter and honey sandwiches, and warm days in the rose garden. Perhaps it was on one of those days that we sat together in the rock garden and she fell abnormally silent, and I couldn't goad her into talking.

A few weeks later, she left for Tripp Lake Camp, run by Caroline Lavenson, to be a counselor. She had begun to suffer again from depression, and Missy and Caroline thought it would be therapeutic for her to be away at camp, distracted from the pressures of being a mother and wife, taking her back to her childhood pleasures. One of the psychotherapists I worked with over the years raised his eyebrows upon hearing this.

"Excuse me?" he said. "She was to leave her child and husband at home and go take care of a group of teenage girls? And this was supposed to be therapeutic for a woman with a major depressive disorder?"

Bad advice as it may have been, everybody seems to have agreed to it. I was left alone with Baba and—when he was there— my father. I was furious with my mother for leaving me alone. She was the sun in my life, as I was supposed to be the sun in hers. She wrote us several times.

> *Dearest Tony:*
>
> *You must be very busy indeed. I've been waiting and waiting for a letter or a card and none comes, but I know that swimming and butterflies and hikes take lots of time. I'm busy too but I'm sending this just to bring my love and a big kiss from Mother.*

> *Darling Kit:*
>
> *I'm so happy that I'm going to see you soon. I know I shall recognize you but I wonder whether you'll know me. I shall probably look very fat and be all decorated with snakes around my neck, turtles in my arms, caterpillars in my hair and butterflies all over me. We go on lots of walks and collect bugs and flowers and frogs and then put them in cages and take care of them. Here is a picture of me to get you used to the idea of your camping mother.*
>
> *Great big hug and ten kisses for my Kit boy, from Mother.*

The letters to Dad are vastly different, and quite painful.

> *July 24, 1941*
> *Darling, oh my darling.*
>
> *While I sit and wait for the call which I fear may not come I shall write you to say what I won't be able to say over the phone—in case the call does come. I had no more intention of suggesting that I didn't want to see you than I had of using*

"slippery phrases" to mislead you. Apparently, like you, I don't know how to express my ideas and feelings so that they are fully understood. What I did mean to suggest was, that having had only 2 letters from you since June 25th, I wondered how much you wanted to see me or hear from me. I've tried so hard to remember how little words mean to you and to believe that you do love and miss me without any overt assurances of it. My only intention in writing you the letter which angered you so was to relieve you of any obligation which, however you might enjoy, would have put an added burden on you. I succeeded only in annoying you, and it's made me very unhappy.

I do love you my darling, I do miss you terribly, I do want to see you and be with you. I do need to know that you want me. I don't want to repeat my so frequent mistakes of forcing you to say and do things which are a strain on you and a drain on your time and energies. Besides all else I'm not as satisfied with my achievements here as my too generous bosses would lead the world to believe. I want to prove to myself that I can do a job and be a really independent person without having to cry out—as I've wanted to—"Oh love me Eddie and in your love protect me from my own lacks and shortcomings!"

The clock ticks on. I think your call won't come.

Your most loving and impatient wife.

I have read these letters from sixty-seven years ago many times. Each reading brings new thoughts and fantasies, as well as a frisson of anxiety.

I have a devout wish that I could reach out to my parents and tell them how wrong they both are about what is happening to them, how much misconstruction and miscomprehension there is in their communications.

My father had known about Francis Froelicher yet kept asking Mother to marry him. He didn't give her time to peel herself away from the other man, to find love anew. What was he trying to prove? That he was the perfect lover? That he could conquer adolescent fantasies? The impossible?

And to my younger self, I want to say, "Your parents are trying. They really are. But circumstances have gotten beyond them."

But, of course, there is no way of reaching back. I have to watch with the perfection of hindsight as they tread water, misconstruing, distrusting, waiting for the waves to take them under.

July 28
Darling.

Thank you for your sweet responsive letter. It means so much to me to spend a few pages with you. And it's what you're thinking, not what you're doing which really fascinates me. Do remember to take in everything that goes on at Treetops. I shall await details avidly. And I'll be awaiting your voice and person early in the afternoon of August 4th.

Elizabeth.

I don't know now how much self-awareness my mother had about her mood, how dark it had turned. I don't know whether the camp personnel knew, either, but I suspect they had been in touch with my father, for after visiting my brother at Treetops on the afternoon of August 3, he continued up the long road to Poland, Maine, picked my mother up, and returned home to White Plains.

During the years leading up to this crisis, Mother constantly fooled people. For those not within the immediate family (and for many who were), she was "beautiful," "charming," "capable," the epitome of grace and happiness. Not once had anyone spoken to me of "desperate, unhappy Elizabeth." "Bipolar Elizabeth." What fools they must have been not to realize that this most beautiful, charming, adequate, talented, happy woman was also capable of killing herself. Did none of them see her as she was: a crushed spirit?

In White Plains, I must have been delighted that she was back, but it was clear by now, to Missy and Dad, that she was seriously depressed. Missy had come up from New York City and—for the next several weeks—took Mother daily to Connecticut, where her new and renowned psychoanalyst, Dr. Herman Nunberg, agreed to see her, even though it was August, the traditional vacation time for analysts.

Meanwhile, terribly concerned that the past might repeat itself, that Mother might attempt to kill herself, Dad consulted Missy's analyst, Bernard Glueck, as well as Mother's brother, Ira, now a physician. Letters and phone calls flew around between Stony Lodge in Ossining, our house in White Plains, and Ira in Ann Arbor. My brother and I were ignorant of the turmoil, though I must have felt the absence of a mother who was physically, though not mentally, at home. In the third week of August, Dad sent a despairing letter to Ira, who responded with caution.

August 21, 1941
Ann Arbor, Michigan
Eddie:

On a number of counts, I would completely oppose any thought of frontal lobotomy for Liza . . . I gather that Nunberg does not consider Liza as great a suicidal risk now that her depression is less deep. If so, I think the best plan is to carry on with the analysis, and hope that Nunberg is right. Shock therapy we can reserve—in our minds—for later, if Liza should not improve sufficiently or have another relapse.

Your unfaltering devotion to Liza through these several diffi-

*cult and trying years fills me with real admiration and respect for
your integrity and courage. I genuinely doubt if I would have
been willing to go through what you have.*

Keep me informed. Ira

There are a number of ironies, sorrows, and shocks surrounding
this letter. The first is that the idea of a *lobotomy* for Mother stuns
me. A procedure that would rob her of her personality, charm,
and wit in return for (possibly) removing her agonizing mood
swings is a bargain that Missy and Dad would, I believe, have
come to regret time and again, no matter how much it might have
preserved Mother's physical being.

In fact, Missy and Dad fought for years over the issue of
whether analysis or shock therapy was the right treatment. Today,
few would recommend psychoanalysis for people with bipolar disorder. Analysis is best for neurotic conflicts, not for biologically
caused mental illnesses, for which today's psychopharmacologists
would prescribe medication. Mother, Dad, Missy, and Ira all had
different ideas about her struggles.

To Mother, her problems were her own "fault," and she
needed to get herself "under control." How each of the others felt
is lost in the ether, but I can guess: a lack of willpower, a neurosis
gone wild, the fault of her upbringing, not to mention tremendous
guilt over her past behavior with, and present thoughts about,
Francis Froelicher.

An irony is that Ira himself was bipolar. Whether he recognized it at this time I don't know, but later he would acknowledge
the disorder and treat it.

Finally, Ira's letter, written on August 21, arrived at White
Plains on the very day that Mother made the last of her daily trips
to visit Dr. Nunberg, the psychoanalyst. It was August 23. She had

gone with Missy as usual—a forty-minute drive up the Hutchinson River Parkway.

Missy decided that she needed to talk to the psychoanalyst to know what he could tell her about Mother's "progress." My grandmother went into Nunberg's office alone and told Mother to wait in the car.

Instead, Mother disappeared in an old greenhouse attached to the doctor's residence. She had brought with her a razor blade, a detail that led people to believe she had intended to harm herself that day. In my view, though, she might simply have made a habit of carrying it with her for when her depression became too great—the kind of "worst-case scenario" preparation that shows itself among the potentially suicidal in the hoarding of sleeping pills. The question for me is, why that day, why that moment? Perhaps it was Missy's insistence on having her own conversation with the doctor. My grandmother was a very intrusive woman; Mother struggled her whole short life to separate herself from Missy, to lead her own, independent life. Whatever the reasons, here, in the stifling damp of the greenhouse, the struggle ended: my mother slashed her wrists and throat.

When Missy and Nunberg came out, they saw that Mother wasn't in the car. Searching for her around the property, they found her body and called an ambulance.

Within half an hour of her arrival at Norwalk Hospital, Mother was dead. The death certificate is painfully terse, typewritten on paper now decades old and crumbling. "Exsanguination," it says, but we know what that means: Mother had *bled out*.

She was thirty-three years old.

AS I LATER DISCOVERED, those who *find* the body have a particularly difficult time recovering from their grief and trauma. So I have thought many times about what it must have been like for my grandmother to discover her own daughter's bleeding body. She and my father had dreaded that such a moment might occur, and now it had. Terror, anger, consternation, guilt, shame. These feelings, plus the most painful sorrow, must have been my grandmother's experience, and my father's lot as well.

Often, I have returned to that event and wondered what lasting effect my mother's suicide had upon the emotions, character, and actions of Missy and Dad over the next decades. Was Dad's accelerated alcoholism due to Mother's suicide? Did Missy's need to control everything around her begin then, too? It seems logical to me that many of the character traits, anxieties, and depressive bouts of everyone who lived around Mother were made worse by her kind of death.

What I do know is that I was not told that Mother was dead. I was told that she was "sick" and that I would have to go away for the night, to my friend Bobby's house.

I can imagine the activity and arguments that were behind that decision. Should we tell Kit? If not, what do we do? It all served a useful purpose—to dam up the horror of the day's events, to create a false calm.

Now they could make practical decisions. Tony, at Camp Treetops already, was booked on for another ten days. I was sent at once to my friend's house. A flurry of phone calls was exchanged between Dad and the owners of the camp, asking if I could be brought there immediately—to get me away from the grief in our house.

Not surprisingly, I don't recall much about what I felt at the time, or thought I knew. I have few memories of that event. I do remember that staying at Bobby Ilgenfritz's house was a big deal, because I'd never slept away from home before. I know I was surprised that my father brought me there, and not Mother, since it had always been Mother who took me places. And I also recall—with a little more sharpness—that I was angry that my mother did not come to say good-bye the next morning when I was driven up to camp.

But beyond that was bewilderment and a series of questions. Was I being sent to Bobby's house because I had been bad? Did my behavior *make* my mother sick? These naive and unanswered questions would inform much of my behavior—and Tony's—for many, many years to come.

THAT NIGHT MY UNCLE, Ira, flew to White Plains airport, and the next morning my father and he drove me the six hours up to camp, to be with Tony.

Along the way to Treetops, it rained. Dad and Ira talked of inconsequential things. I, only six years old and frightened of the strange turn of events, sat in the backseat, dumb and virtually ignored. While I knew nothing of the disaster we were leaving behind, I cannot understand how the two of *them* avoided dropping in their tracks from the pressure. Halfway there we passed a flatbed truck carrying part of a house that had literally been sawed in two. A little farther on was the other half. Did Dad and Ira even see the unavoidably personal symbol it later came to represent to me: a world cut in two?

Arriving at Treetops in the evening, I was put to bed in a room all by myself. Ira and Dad promised to visit me in the morning. For now, though, I was alone. My mother had not said good-bye to me. She, who was always to be by my side, comforting me when things got tough, had simply disappeared. I cried myself to sleep.

In the morning Tony came to my room. He didn't ask questions, simply taking me by the hand to the staircase. Alongside the stairs was a long, curving wooden slide on which the braver kids descended from the second floor to the first. I was enchanted by it and gave it a try. Then another, and another. Tony had to drag me to breakfast.

Later in the day, I wrote and mailed a letter. "Dear Mommy," I said, "I don't like it here. I want to come home." Dad and Ira came by, as promised, but then said they had to go. By now, with Tony as my protector and guide, I was sufficiently secure to let them leave. But that night I cried my eyes out again. How was I to interpret this abandonment by the one person with whom I had experienced such joy for six years?

But children can be resilient, and as the ten days passed, in which my main memory is of sunshine, bad food, and carpentry shop, the lonely nights, fear, and bewilderment began to fade.

Had the recriminations already begun down there in White Plains? Were they arguing over how to tell us about Mother's death? Were Missy and Dad fighting over who was at fault in this terrible no-win war? Should they have gone back to shock therapy? Should they have kept a "suicide watch"? Should they have trusted the psychoanalyst?

Dad once told me that he spoke to Dr. Nunberg shortly after Mother's death, to try to glean a hint of how this event had not been foreseen. The doctor said, "How could she do this to *me?*"

Dad was horrified, but said nothing to reprimand him.

But wasn't that what they all were thinking? How could this beautiful, sweet, talented woman desert me? Shame me. Anger me. Make me feel guilty. Make me fear for my own life.

Ten days after Mother's suicide, Tony and I came home, and Dad met us at the train station. I was six and Tony was eight. Normally, if either of us had been anywhere, it was Mother who picked us up. This experience was again *not normal.* I had never been to sleepaway camp, nor had I been absent from the house for more than a night. It was all strange, and the fact that Mother was not there made it even stranger.

"Where's my mother?" I asked as Dad opened the car door for us.

"I'll tell you in the car," he said.

Once we were on our way, I asked again.

Dad said, "You remember that your mother was sick when you left?"

I nodded.

"Well, she died."

I turned toward the backseat and said to Tony, "Don't believe him. He's just kidding."

"No," said my father. "I'm not kidding."

His face was solemn, but there were no tears, no quivering voice. I began to cry, and as I looked back at Tony, there was moistness in his eyes, but he did not sob or weep. Dad asked if we wanted him to pull over to the side of the road so we could cry. We said no. We wanted to go home. Maybe we'd find out he was wrong about Mother.

When my own young children wept, I found it impossible not to sweep them up into my arms and comfort them. Even today—they are in their thirties—I would find it impossible not to hug them if they were in pain. I do not recall any such behavior on my father's part—not then, not in subsequent weeks. Maybe my memory is faulty. Tony never did remember the events of those years, so he was no help. But I recall that we all froze in place, and only I gave way to the emotion of the moment.

As we reached our house, I ran inside, shouting to anyone who would listen: "My mother's dead. My mother's dead." Of course, they knew it. They knew it beyond reason and doubt.

It would be ten years before we learned the truth.

During those years, Dad never spoke about Mother. Nor did anyone else. It was as if she hadn't existed. Tony and I were well-behaved little boys. We should have attended a memorial service where we could mourn and share our grief with others. We should have been given a chance to say *good-bye*. We *should* have been asking, "How *did* Mother die?" We didn't ask, because that's the way the adults seemed to want it. To some this may seem difficult to believe. How could two children *not* inquire what had happened to their mother—so mysteriously there one day and not the next? The answer lies in the tenacity of my father's game plan to "protect" us (and himself) from the terrible experience, in the lie itself ("she died because she was sick"), which was so bland as to be believable, and, finally, in our wish to be good and careful and silent, so that bad things wouldn't happen again. But underneath, at least for me, the questions kept coming. Answers did not come.

AS SUMMERS END, I reflect on the several anniversaries that are coming up: the suicide on August 23; the return from Tripp Lake Camp in early September.

I was taught from childhood to be a *rational* man.

I do not believe in astrological signs.

I do not avoid black cats or leaning ladders.

I laugh when the elevator passes the twelfth floor and comes next to fourteen.

I try to organize my life around what I can see, what I can hold in my hands, what I can prove.

And yet—

I believe deeply in anniversaries.

OF THE NEXT TWELVE MONTHS, I have almost no memory. My psychiatrist later said that it was some kind of defensive fugue—an attempt to garrison myself against feelings of helplessness and despair, not to mention intense rage, at my mother's disappearance. I just could not comprehend it. No one took the time to tell me of her illness and angst. It was considered too grown-up a discussion to have with a six-year-old boy (or, for that matter, with Tony, an eight-year-old). As a consequence, I went through a series of painful question-and-answer sessions within myself: "Why me?" and "What if?" and "What did I do?" questions. The answers were all unpalatable, full of self-blame and self-doubt; I finally put them away, deep into my unconscious. I do not know what Tony thought or felt. Years later, when we could finally discuss these matters, my brother professed no recollection of the events preceding or immediately following Mother's death. Nor did he indicate any desire to pursue the subject. It was, he insisted, another indication of my "preoccupation" with death. To my mind, *not* tackling the subject, continuing to shove it out of his consciousness, left Tony vulnerable to a barrage of feelings that sandbagged him over and over again.

In 1941, Missy quickly took over the household. She stayed for a year, bringing with her an I-am-always-right attitude. Missy had firmly dominated Mother's activities and behaviors until—judging by her letters from Europe—Elizabeth struggled and then *did* pull clear of my grandmother's taffy-like grasp, finding both freedom and madness. It was a struggle with control and self-control with which I can empathize. I also found myself torn between Missy's overprotective grip and freedom.

I can think of no better demonstration of her sense of rectitude and her need to control than a story told me by Ira. In 1933, before Mother had been so ill, Ira had entered medical school and was studying for his first year's big exams. Missy, always concerned for his health because of his youthful tuberculosis, wrote and suggested that he accompany her to Marblehead for a week, so she could make sure he was well.

"You need a rest," she said.

He replied, "I have exams. I can't go."

A day later, she arrived at Johns Hopkins and told him that she had talked to the dean, who said it was okay for him to take the examinations when he came back.

Imagine them, then, the twenty-three-year-old Ira and his forty-eight-year-old mother, up in beautiful Marblehead, sunning on the beach, eating good food. Ira loved to sail, and I can envision him out on his own (Missy wouldn't go near the boats) in one of the sloops of his day, taking in the sylvan coastline, letting the boat heel over against his touch on the tiller, doing the balancing act that all sailors do: between speed and safety. Perhaps he experienced frustration at his mother's insistence that he turn in early—as did I, twenty years later. Perhaps he felt embarrassed when she told him to wear a sweater, or suggested he meet that "nice girl" at the table next to them.

After a week, refreshed, ready to take his exams, Ira returned to Johns Hopkins only to learn that he had been failed for not taking his finals. He rushed to see the dean.

"But my mother . . . ," he explained.

Actually, Missy had never talked to the dean. Luckily, when that august personage learned what had happened, he allowed Ira to take makeup examinations. And Ira had that story to add to his list of Missy tales.

MISSY BROUGHT WITH HER ANNA FUCHS, the refugee from Nazi-occupied Czechoslovakia. Conversant in several languages, this tall, thin woman with a craggy Slavic face served to guide and protect Tony and myself; we were both desperately in need of a friendly and understanding person to watch over us. Baba was there, too, but more and more it was Anna and Missy who were our guardians.

That next summer Dad sent us off to camp while he wrestled with financial matters. Then, coughing violently and feeling weak, he went for a chest X-ray. Tuberculosis was diagnosed. While we were still away at camp, he underwent a pneumothorax operation. One of his lungs had become so infected the physicians needed to deflate it—to allow it to recover. The operation left Dad weak.

What hurt the most for Dad was not the pain or the disease but that he had just started work at the Society for the Prevention of Crime. The Society was formed in the mid-nineteenth century to shut down porno shops and houses of prostitution. By the time Dad got there, however, it had a formidable board of advisers, including the director of federal prisons, professors, judges, and important public figures in New York City. By the 1940s, the Society had changed its goals from trying to prevent crime to trying to prevent *criminals*, a vastly different and equally difficult—if not impossible—enterprise.

Dad signed on with great enthusiasm.

Now, however, just as this exciting work was beginning, he was forced to leave the Society for a "cure" in a TB sanitarium.

He had lost his wife and his health, and he would soon have to sell his home. He had some hard decisions to make, including what to do with us while he was away. He knew one thing: he wanted us to be anywhere *but* with Missy, who had offered to take us with her to New York City and send us to public school there. Dad would have none of that. He and Missy had been violently in disagreement on what treatment to give Mother. They each felt that her suicide was the result of leaning too heavily on the *wrong* therapy. This sad conclusion on their part caused rifts between them that disrupted all our lives for years. When Dad had to go away for treatment, it was impossible for him to ignore the consequences he foresaw if he "gave us over" to Missy.

He decided to sell the house and send us to Vermont, to the Putney School, a boarding school that Mother had learned about years earlier. Missy was appalled. In a series of letters, Dad tried to explain to Ira, who was now in a public service job in New Orleans, why he was sending us away to school despite Missy's "kind offer" to harbor us.

These letters have always struck me as remarkably obfuscatory; he clearly wanted to keep his feelings from his brother-in-law. The letters are also remarkable for the formality of style, so very different from Mother's free flow of thought.

July 28, 1942
Dear Ira:

It was good of you to phone last night.

I want to reassure you on one point. MBS is one of the most generous and thoughtful people I ever knew. Her motives are always unimpeachable; her desire to be helpful can never be questioned.

Were this all, I should have no hesitancy in saying that my mind would be free of the concern over the welfare of the children during my enforced inactivity for the coming year. But, simultaneously, she is the victim of a tremendous drive which manifests itself in an unpredictable fashion; her highly neurotic reactions to situations, especially as concerns the children, charges the atmosphere with a kind of electric hecticity that results in an unevenness of routine, to say nothing of the basic unevenness in the degree and manifestations of devotion toward one as contrasted with the other. In this connection, I want to emphasize "manifestations," because, in the last analysis, it is natural for a person to feel more affection and sympathy toward T or K; and it would be unnatural for us to expect M or anyone else to feel essentially the same toward both. However, it is against the demonstration *of any difference in feeling that I object.*

There may also be a hangover from our differences in relations to E's illness; but I won't go into that now, and I have never discussed that subject with her since that fateful conference last August.

I am determined to become well, even if I become broke in the process.

The other side of the coin: Missy writes to Dad.

Dear Eddie:

I hope your convalescence will be less tedious and swifter than you anticipate. Since I realize that my personality does produce conflicts, it seems the better part of wisdom to remove it. If you want me at any time or if I can be of any use to you or the children, remember I am standing by.

Affectionately,

May

Both of these letters are extraordinarily disingenuous. Dad never felt that Missy's generosity was authentic, and I often heard him rail against her motives. There is a story that she offered to adopt me at one point, which left Dad apoplectic. As for Missy, she always felt that Dad was an unfeeling man and that only she could take proper care of us.

Yet what strikes me most, every time I read these letters, is a recurrent fear of mine that Dad did indeed feel differently toward Tony than toward me. In fact, I never believed that he loved me, or thought me as smart or as diligent or as "important" as Tony. When he shouted at me or reprimanded me ("Don't run so fast!"

"Can't you sit still?" "How many times do I have to tell you?"), I was sure he was doing it with more passion or with a greater degree of anger than with Tony.

Perhaps he would have been shocked to hear that I felt singled out. Perhaps it was simply my own miserable self-doubt and insecurity that painted this portrait. Perhaps Dad loved us both equally, or came to love us both equally.

Or none of the above. Children's feelings about parents are complex, and I do not pretend to be so "analyzed" that I can ever totally sort mine out. For years, I had very angry feelings toward Dad. I believed that he had taken Mother away from me—on purpose.

Missy did favor some of her grandchildren over others and was not able—or willing—to hide it. When cousins and grandchildren assembled for the holidays, she sometimes gave gifts to one or another of us that were radically different in value. She saw no harm in this. She showered affection on me openly. And I responded with delight. Tony, who could never bring himself to offer Missy the unfettered "I love you" that she required, was treated to a different level of affection: reasonable, but not unconditional. Of course, her love for me was not really unconditional. As I grew and (at a late age) finally pulled myself from the relationship, I realized that my grandmother needed my complete and undivided attention. She did not want to let me go. Ever.

Was Tony wise to cut himself off from her right at the beginning? Or was he unable to control how he behaved? Until I began to reflect on our past, I did not think deeply about how my brother might have felt being the odd man out. I had assumed that he was glad not to be at Missy's beck and call, pleased to be free to remain shut up in our room, reading a good book, while I went into the living room to listen to the piano or into her bedroom to chat with her and answer whatever probing questions she had. When Missy said, "A penny for your thoughts," it wasn't a casual statement. She was perfectly willing to pay—in candy, money, a movie, a new coat or sled—as long as I was willing to tell her what I was thinking about.

But did Tony feel slighted? Was his withdrawal actually not a welcome release but the reaction of a hurt little boy? What, in short, if he was showing not insensitivity to Missy but a great deal of sensitivity?

Back in 1942, there were no such questions, no such thoughts. What I know now is that, despite Missy's firm grasp on me—and the battles it caused with Dad—I came through my childhood as well as I did because Missy cared and took care of me.

In 1942, however, Tony and I mourned the loss of our White Plains home. Someday, we knew, when we were grown, we would buy the house at 250 Rosedale Avenue—and live there happily ever after.

Chapter Five

Kit, Edwin, and Tony Lukas, 1939

IF TUBERCULOSIS WAS DAD'S WORST NEWS, the most severe blow to Tony and me was that, for the second year in a row, a parent was ill and would leave us. And we would leave him. Who knew what might follow?

Anna told us not to show our grief: "Your father needs all the sympathy he can get." It was the only bad advice she ever gave me. In retrospect, it seems to me that *we* needed all the sympathy *we* could get. At the ages of seven and nine, we had already lost our mother to a mysterious death, our father was ill and going away, our home was being sold, and we were being sent two hundred miles away to a place we'd never heard of, to be taken care of by people who were total strangers.

As if I didn't have enough anxiety and distress, when the appointed time to go came Tony had a cold and couldn't go with me. He had to stay in bed for at least a week, the doctor said. A cold! How sick does that make a young boy? Why couldn't he still go with me? Why couldn't I wait until he was well? No one ever answered those questions. Again, I felt betrayed.

In 1935 the progressive educator Carmelita Hinton bought Elm Lea—a four-hundred-acre cattle and hay farm on the top of East Hill—to establish the Putney School. Based on ideas she had gleaned from John Dewey, the regimen included eighty-minute academic classes, work on the farm, heavy emphasis on the arts, attention to politics. Putney started with a few dozen students and became nationally known as the benchmark of a well-rounded, "progressive" co-ed education, in which graduates were urged to solve the problems of the world as humanitarians, not just as scholars. Mrs. Hinton was the widow of the man who had invented the jungle gym, thereby providing enough money when he died to start the school. Sebastian Hinton had killed himself, but none of us learned that until many years later. Mrs. Hinton's younger brother, Phil, started a school for the elementary grades a few miles away, and it was actually to that branch of Putney—called Hickory Ridge—that we were going.

Missy took me up to Putney and waited with me until Tony was well. For the first of nearly a hundred times over the next ten years, I climbed aboard a train at Grand Central and headed up the Connecticut valley to Vermont. As we went into the train, carrying just a small suitcase (the trunk would follow by Railway Express), I was comforted by the fact that my grandmother was with me, but I was terrified at what lay ahead. I did not really understand what a boarding school was, except that there would be all sorts of strangers, including boys older than I who might want to hurt me or tease me, and that my brother would not be there to protect me. And that my mother and father were—for all practical purposes—gone, vanished.

Still, it must have been somewhat exciting to look out at the passing scenery as city gave way to town and town gave way to countryside. I found the world outside those windows vastly fascinating. Fields that stretched wide across flatlands and long sheds with tin roofs and slatted sides. These held tobacco, drying in the sun and fresh air.

On future trips on the Cigar Valley Express, when we traveled alone, comic books became our solace. They reminded us that crime didn't pay, that crooks and Nazis could be caught, that right always wins—*and that lost little boys are always reclaimed.* Comic books showed us that it was possible—if only in fantasy—to turn oneself from a weakling into a powerful force for good, a force that could twist its way into nooks and crannies, fly to distant spots, pierce solid substances, and always—*always*—triumph. For two little boys caught in the spiderweb of a world gone mad, they were an essential part of our survival kit.

When Missy and I arrived at the Putney station in mid-September 1942, we found the village's sole taxi waiting. It was a short drive up from the river to the town, which had been founded in 1753, long before Vermont became a state.

The population in the town of Putney those days was small, but it was a wonderful place to learn about America. There were three churches—one Catholic, and two of Protestant denominations. There was a village hall, where the town selectmen met monthly and where, in true democratic fashion, a town meeting was held on the second Tuesday of every March. All laws had to pass before every voting adult. In the evening on Town Meeting day, a square dance was held, and to the delight of the children hot maple syrup, fresh from the local, wood-fired sugarhouses, would be poured over pure snow. The instantly crystallized sweet was as good a treat as any I have ever had. Black coffee, pickles, and plain donuts were offered to soften the potential shock to our systems of so much sugar.

After our five-hour train ride, the coal dust was too clotted in our nostrils, and Missy too agitated, to go right up to the school. It is hard sometimes to realize that, despite her regal and controlled manner, Missy had only recently lost a daughter and that now—as she saw it—she was losing her favorite grandson. She had dared; she had asked to have us with her in New York and, having been refused that, must have felt both angry and bereft. Having a child die by suicide is both an accusation and an irretrievable loss. But since Tony and I had suffered our own losses, we didn't think about her.

Knowing there would not be accommodations befitting her at Hickory Ridge (outdoor plumbing was still in use that first fall), Missy had booked a bed-and-breakfast halfway up the hill above the village, just next to the co-op food store. The pleasant owner of that B and B was a longtime resident who welcomed us with a cup of tea for Missy, a cookie for me, and a comfortable cot in Missy's room for me to rest on. I lay there for a while, in fitful daydreams of what awaited me, but soon fell asleep.

When I woke, it was dark, and I could see that Missy's bed was empty. In fact, it had not been slept in. Thus began a recurrent shudder of fear that I was being abandoned again. In later years, that terror would send me to the bathroom with an instant case of stomach cramps. That night it simply propelled me into action: out the door, down the stairs, looking for my grandmother. She was nowhere in sight. I opened the front door, and a voice called to me from the kitchen. It was our landlady.

"Have you seen my grandmother?" I sniffled.

"She went out for a walk, darling," the woman said.

"Oh . . ."

"She'll be back soon. Do you want to sit here with me until she comes back." I debated. Was the cold kitchen chair a place I wanted to wait, or the comfortable cot upstairs? I chose the cot, but I didn't go to sleep until my grandmother came back and went to bed.

The next morning we took a taxi to Hickory Ridge. It was the middle of September and the leaves were that dark summer green that comes with ample sun and water. Up toward the top of the hills, a few had begun to turn into the rust and gold that, within a month, would flood the landscape with unparalleled beauty. But even if they were already brilliant, I doubt that I would have seen them. Though the streams were full of sparkling water and the hills full of verdant growth, my heart was beating wildly. I feared what lay ahead.

The road was made of packed dirt. We climbed for twenty minutes, and then came out on a clearing where a large yellow farmhouse had been modified to accommodate thirty student rooms. Carpenters were working on a dining-room/kitchen addition. A large red barn was nearby, and I could hear horses neighing in the paddock. We were directed to a small machine shed where Helen Chase, the headmaster's wife, was preparing lunch in a makeshift kitchen. Missy showed her how to mix peanut butter and honey in a big bowl and spread the premixed mess on bread, rather than doing each slice individually. Mrs. Chase was grateful. Missy had asked the taxi to wait, and now set back off for town, saying she'd come by tomorrow. Who knows what was in her heart? I can only guess that she was dismayed to be leaving me behind, distraught that Dad had chosen to send a seven-year-old boy into this wilderness rather than leave him with her in the safety of her New York apartment. Later, I could understand why he had done what he had done. But at the moment I felt far from protected.

I cried. Mrs. Chase chastised me. "I don't like little boys who cry," she said. I stopped crying, but I never learned to like her, not in the six years that I spent at Hickory Ridge.

When Tony finally caught up with me, a week later, we were bedded down in the same room. The theory was that he could comfort me when I got too frightened or sad. And indeed, years later, Tony told me that he listened to my crying after lights-out as I revisited the pain that had been set upon us. I desperately wanted him to tell me everything was going to be okay, but I don't remember that happening, ever.

I would not let my brother out of my sight for long. As far as I knew, he was the only family member I still had. I did more than keep an eye on him: I strove to protect him from every possible ill. On cookouts, which were frequent, I made sure he had his food first. When classes were over for the day, I rushed to find him, to make sure he was okay. This proved to be an annoyance to Tony. It was bad enough having a younger brother tagging after him, but a seven-year-old who turned the tables and tried to take care of a nine-year-old was infuriating. The pattern was set for years to come: I was concerned about him; he did not seem to be concerned about me.

America had entered World War II. Big-time. Outside, in the "real world," ration cards were issued; travel by car or train was limited; censorship was established. And millions of young men enlisted in the various branches of the armed forces, determined to throw Hitler and Tōjō from their thrones of power. Because we were isolated in this little Vermont town, we were spared some of the frightening aspects of wartime America: the brownouts, when all lights had to be hidden from view at night; air-raid siren testing; the establishment of air-raid shelters; talk of invasions or shelling from offshore submarines.

And so, despite the fears that came at night, there were times at the school when we forgot that we had been sent into the wilderness. Exiled from parents, from comfort, from everything that "home" had meant to us—the excitement and freedom of boarding school life finally took over our spirits.

In the winter, we all went skiing—a mandatory sport. Those early skis were long and cumbersome, with spring bindings that didn't come loose when we fell. The poles, made of bamboo, came up to our armpits. Tony and I took to the slopes with gusto, but not with great skill. Later, I worked my way up to become a ski instructor and once won a downhill race against another school. But in general, I was not a speedster on the slopes, nor did I try ski jumping. I might have been graceful, but I was not courageous.

Tony was never graceful; he was, in fact, ungainly. His arms and hands were carried forward of his body, not smoothly, but in jerks, rising and falling as his body twisted in an attempt to perform acts of physical skill. His body was out of rhythm, his legs pumping almost spasmodically. When he skied, he *threw* himself down the slope, his upper body trying to wrest his lower body into turns rather than melting into the slope as the best skiers do. At soccer he churned down the field, his lips taut, his brow furrowed, trying to reach, to kick the twirling ball, often as not sending it far afield from his desired target. Only when he played second base or shortstop did his longtime love of the game of baseball enable him to fire a hardball straight to first, angling for a double play. The rest of the time—at other sports—he was lucky if he just got the job done.

However, in his face you could see the effort, the intensity, the will to succeed. With his eyes bulging, his lips tightly compressed, you couldn't tell if he was angry or just concentrating on the job.

I often thought he would fall onto the playing field or the slope out of sheer exertion or desperation to get it right, but he entered into sports and theater and even square dancing with a gusto reminiscent of the way in which he had bitten into an onion sandwich as a child, or the way in which he tackled his homework. For him, it was all or nothing.

His lack of grace extended to his personal appearance. Tony did not wear clothes well. Even when, after his marriage, he bought the finest shirts and double-breasted jackets, there was something sloppy about the way he stood—hands crammed in his pants pockets, one hip lower than the other, his tie ever so slightly askew. Perhaps it was an image from that play about journalism in the ôld days, *The Front Page*, a jacket-off, shirtsleeves-rolled-up look, that attracted him. Or maybe he was just clumsy of body, the way he was elegant of intellect.

Life at Hickory Ridge was harsh at first. The walls were full of leaks and took the full brunt of winter snows and autumn rains. In the middle of the night, wind screeched past the faulty caulking around our windows. It entered into our beds—the radiators having long since ceased their whistling warmth—and we wriggled in our deep sleep, feeling the chill. In the morning, we slipped on long johns, ran down the hall to the newly installed bathroom, and hastily washed our faces before descending to a stomach-warming breakfast of Cream of Wheat.

Tony was no more fit to the north country than I, but the fact that he was two years older gave him a leg up on adaptation to cold and wind. While we both would learn to deal with winter chills and rough lodging, in those first two years I didn't adapt to the emotional cold.

Lying in bed, I tried to convince myself that I had concocted all this squalor. It was merely a movie of my life, over which I had control as some future film director, or, at the worst, a phantasm of loneliness and discomfort, not real life. But I remember distinctly that this did not, in the end, comfort me. The "movie" didn't end; no fairy godmother came floating out of the sky. Only the headmaster, Phil, his crinkled, leathery Vermont face bending over the bed, coaxing me back to sleep, but promising a life of unease for years to come.

Nonetheless, I formulated one firm idea: if I behaved like the good little boy everyone said I was (and that I knew I wasn't; otherwise, why would my mother and father have abandoned me and sent me off into the freezing hell of Vermont?), *eventually* my mother would return.

If not my mother, then surely my father would come here, make amends for his inept handling of my childhood, compensate us for the pain and sorrow. He would take us into his home, into his bosom, and pay us back for what had been stolen from us.

AT HICKORY RIDGE, Tony began the intellectual and physical growth spurt that would take him to Harvard and the *New York Times*. Even his first report card makes the point. He is nine years old. Elizabeth Hamill, his English teacher, writes: "Tony is a very conscientious worker. His script is beautiful. His creative writing shows both thinking and originality and a happy feeling for the poetry in language." And his history teacher, Ida Belle Hegemann, pens: "Tony is attentive and rather quiet in history class. His questions are always pertinent, which shows that he is interested in the subject. His comprehension is good and he gave a well thought-out talk in a history assembly. His papers are written with care and thought, and with attention to sentence structure."

They did not think the same about me. For ten years, I followed in his footsteps, academically, with the same courses, the same teachers; my footprint was never as big as his. "If only Kit would work harder," they said. "You never quite live up to your potential," one teacher wrote me directly. I was "scattered" in my organization.

Of course, as I look back on it, we both had our strengths. I was easy to get along with. I had a spontaneous, almost instinctive sense of music, an inborn ear. Though I never became the professional conductor I aspired to be, I have always been able to enjoy all kinds of music and performing arts. And, unlike Mother, who complained of her "over-quick mind," I found it enjoyable to make quick decisions, to get on with things, whether they were profound or not. Some things, after all, do not demand perfection or a lifetime to decide.

One of those things was acting. At Hickory Ridge, I quickly entered the world of drama, performing plays like *Toad of Toad Hall*: efforts to encourage elementary school children to express themselves. I needed no encouragement. Mother's plays on the window seat had prepared me. I loved the exposure to an audience. I loved approbation. Though I always wanted to be the hero, the serious one, it was with comedy that I began to win not only applause but laughter—and I loved it.

WE WAITED FOR DAD to let us know when—if ever—he would be coming home. At Thanksgiving, that first year, we rode the sooty train to New York and stayed with Missy. The same occurred at Christmas. We conversed with Dad over the long-distance phone. He was in Phoenix, Arizona, at a tuberculosis sanitarium. He was getting better, he said.

Our X-rays—taken before we left for school—were fine; only *he* had the disease. He hoped to be back within a year.

A year! That seemed like an eternity to me. How would I survive? What would happen to me—and to Tony? I was on terra incognita.

Children are resilient, or at least they *appear* to be. Looking back, I cannot be sure which was true of me, or of Tony. At the time, we appeared to go on with normal children's lives—if "normal" can include seven- and nine-year-olds being sent two hundred miles away to a raw country life to live with strangers. But we did play and learn, and enjoy the benefits of a Vermont lifestyle.

Underneath, however, I was coming to terms, in a very strange way, with the notion that my mother was dead and my father had gone away.

In the spring of 1943, Dad showed up at school. He had returned only recently from Arizona and was eager to get to work again at the Society for the Prevention of Crime, pursuing his holy grail: preventing delinquents from growing up into adult criminals.

When he came up to Hickory Ridge, Dad was thirty pounds heavier than the last time we'd seen him; he didn't look like himself. Clearly, the bed rest, fattening foods, and other treatment at the sanitarium had improved his health. But when he left, I confided to Tony that I did not believe this man was our father. This was a trick that was being played on us. Our *real* father was still in Arizona, with Mother. We would never see either of them again. Tony looked askance at me, but did not tell anyone what I had said.

My head was filled with nightmares. Just after Mother's death, I dreamed of being buried alive. I would wake in a terror. Later, in adolescence and early adulthood, evildoers were after me, chasing me with spears. Luckily, I could fly, and I would hover just above their raised weapons, fleeing, just out of reach. In adulthood, the most intense dreams have been ones in which some beautiful girl or woman abandons me or is simply out of reach: she remains silent, never contacting me or letting me contact her. It was a video replay I could not turn off. The machine was on automatic.

Clearly, I was not happy, and I was not particularly stable. Shortly after the visit from Dad, I started setting fires in wastebaskets in teachers' rooms. I always put them out, but soon Phil Chase, the head of the school, and others noticed and started trying to figure out who was doing this dangerous trick. One evening,

Phil sat me down in his tiny office and asked me to tell him whether I was in fact the arsonist. I admitted it. To my surprise, he was not angry. He sympathized with my fears and my grief. He knew I wasn't happy. He asked for my cooperation in helping him keep the place safe. I had to say yes, and in fact I was pleased to do so. At last, I had received real comfort, real understanding.

Eight times a year, Tony and I took that train between Putney and New York. We grew physically and intellectually. On vacations, Tony and I did things together, but seldom at school, where I continued to inquire if he had had enough to eat, gotten enough sleep, wanted to go to the soccer game. I was still trying to reassure myself that he, too, wouldn't get sick and abandon me, that I knew where he was at all times. He, however, found the attention anything but gratifying and sought out boys his own age for company. In my eighth-grade year, he was no longer there, having moved up from Hickory Ridge to Putney, three miles away. I had to find friends to supplant him.

I gravitated to Tom Russell, whom we called Rusty, with his golden hair falling constantly across his freckled face, stocky legged, running across the soccer field, or taking off—soaring— into the air from the ski jump. His parents had moved the family to India when he was very young, and he and his sister grew up attended by amahs and watching cobras drink milk from straw bowls. It was the era of the Raj, and when the Rockefellers came visiting their Standard Oil domain, Tom's father (who was their manager for India, Burma, China, and Ceylon) showed them around. The war came; Tom, his sister, and their mother were sent home. Somewhere in Ceylon, Tom's father got killed by the Japanese.

Tom would sit, cross-legged, his calves bulging under the strain, clutching a dog-eared paperback close to his chest so we couldn't see the pages, and read to us, the hungry looks on our faces telling him how much we wanted him to go on.

She came towards me, her breasts heaving. "I want you," she said, letting her dress fall noiselessly to the floor.

The book snapped shut. Rusty heaved himself up out of his cramped position and went to play soccer or sun himself in back of our dormitory. The book was put away in a Chinese puzzle box that my other roommate and I could never open. I don't know why we allowed ourselves to be toyed with like that, but then, we were only twelve years old, and it's not hard for one preteen with lots of worldly experience to fool another.

It wasn't until the end of the year that I finally got a glimpse at that book. It was a Penguin edition of *The Scarlet Pimpernel*, and the closest there was to a seduction scene was in the name of the book. But there was something about Tom, about his seductive voice, his unbearable masculinity, that made the story believable, and every time he "read" us excerpts, our mouths watered, our tiny penises rose beneath our sheltering hands, and we begged him for more. I suppose it was natural, then, that I should have fallen in love with Tom, natural for me, that is, a boy whose brother didn't pay him much attention, who made him feel small.

Not that I ever let on, of course. We were chaste and platonic as could be, much as my mother apparently had been with Frances Berwanger. And soon, when Tom and I both went up to Putney, I began to focus on girls. Soon, too, because he was a superb baseball player, Tom would be taken up by the boys one or two classes ahead of us. He became very close to Tony, and the three of us would occasionally vacation in New York or go to a ball game.

IN THE SPRING OF 1945, as the war wound down (I was ten, Tony twelve), we got word at Hickory Ridge that Dad had remarried. The new wife was a tall, stunning redhead named Ruth West who worked in advertising at J. Walter Thompson. She had a daughter, Piri, from her first marriage.

I was elated. This would mean we had a new mother, someone to look after us and give us what we'd been missing for four years. Tony was more cautious. This was our father's new wife, not necessarily a new mother for us. I don't think he was actually eager to have a new mother. His experience of the old one had been less than stellar. *I* was eager for a reincarnation.

In some ways, this characterized a major difference between us. I was hopeful (though not always optimistic) that life could take a wonderful turn for the better, almost magically. Tony was confident that nothing could create good outcomes except hard work, diligence, and attention to detail. If mine was a fantastical way of looking at the world—one that was bound to have many disappointments—his would leave him disenchanted before the battle even began.

For that summer's vacation in 1945 we all settled into a house in Larchmont, a suburb of New York City. It was the first summer we had not gone to camp or stayed with Missy, and I thought it might prove to be the beginning of a permanent structure for our disjointed lives. But the only permanence was the house itself, one of those fake-English, half-timbered buildings on a quiet side street.

The summer is memorable for two things: Tony and I actually spent lots of time together, riding bicycles down the back roads to Mount Vernon, taking tin cans and newspapers to the collection dump "for the war effort," and trying to get used to the idea of a sister and a new mother.

But the big event occurred when Tony discovered Jack, a boy his own age. Not only did Jack engage in the wartime practice of collecting tin cans and tinfoil for the government to do whatever it did with such stuff, but he loved *baseball*. Why did he love the game? Because his father was the lawyer for the radio station WINS, which broadcast the Yankee games.

If a fairy godmother had come down and given Tony three wishes, they could not have been more exciting or fulfilling than the next thing that happened.

"I don't suppose you'd like to go meet Mel Allen and sit in the radio booth, would you?" asked the cherub from down the block.

Allen was the Southern-born "voice of the Yankees." He had a deep, mellow tone and was someone who could describe the minutiae of activity on the field without once losing sight of the larger picture. I remember hearing him tell in great detail how a particular pitcher was preparing to throw, and realized even then how Allen's use of words entranced Tony.

The trip to Yankee Stadium was a triumph for Tony. Jack's father procured four tickets to the next game. Tony, Jack, Jack's father, and I went. At the appropriate moment, we went up to the broadcast booth, met Mel Allen, sat in the booth, got autographs, and went back to our seats. The Yankees won. The Sox lost. It was not the first game Tony had been to, but it was one of the most memorable. Tony adored baseball, but he loved the descriptive power of words, too. Mel Allen, with his roaring "How about that!" when something startling or exciting or devastating happened during a game, was the stuff of myth and history and had given baseball radio the power to generate images.

My brother's relationship with baseball was intense. In later years, after he had shut me out of his amateur playing, I think he regretted that I knew so little about it. When we attended games at Yankee Stadium, he was constantly bewildered and slightly angered by the fact that I didn't understand arcane subjects such as the infield fly rule.

"Jesus, Kit, if you don't know that one by now, you'll never learn it."

Years before, Proctor had reserved for Tony the supreme privilege of learning how to throw a baseball and how to hit. Once Tony had gotten the rudiments of the game, he badgered Proctor to take any and every spare moment from household duties to engage in practice. Above the Rosedale Avenue garage was Proctor's bedroom. There, he had a radio and listened to ball games whenever he could. Tony was allowed to go there, listen with him, and learn the rudiments.

As a player, Tony learned to throw fast to second for an attempted double play. And while, as I've suggested, he was not especially agile or talented, his fierce interest in the game put him on teams. At Putney, where baseball was a hardball, interschool game, he didn't make varsity until his senior year. By then, he was already filled with the statistics and jargon of baseball, and in some ways I don't think it really mattered to him whether he played on the Putney team or not. He had already *experienced* the big time—in the broadcast booth, and in his mind.

He would write about baseball only occasionally, but in my view one particular exegesis of the sport is an example of his writing at its best, because it gets into his personal thoughts and feelings. It's in a collection called *Birth of a Fan*, in which the editor, Ron Fimrite, put together a bunch of writers who wrote about how and why they became enamored of sports. In a piece titled "Surrogate Family," Tony spilled his emotions out onto the page, revealing for the first time how important it was for him to listen to baseball on the radio.

For years, Tony and I had no permanent home, no family fireside. In place of that—as he saw it—there was that first radio, stashed in Proctor's bedroom, and then another old radio, in the workshop of Putney's carpenter, a tall, grizzled Vermonter named Tom Morse. There, as Tony and his friends pretended to do what were called "work jobs" in the spring afternoons at school, they listened to the Red Sox and the Yankees duke it out on Tom's radio, twisting the antenna this way and that to get the signal clear. In his essay, Tony spelled out the relationship of those players and the listeners to *him*: they were the family he never had, the brotherhood that *could* exist; the power of the bat and the ball, the swift throw, the clean out, the sense of manhood. It was a world free from women who might either abandon him or—as with Missy— try to rule with a fierce hand.

To Tony, sliding home was not metaphor but reality. A "home run" was what he ached for, and Tony found it in Tom Morse's workshop. As he would write in "Surrogate Family":

> Baseball reaches something deep inside me, stirring the guttering embers of memory and feeling. It keeps me in touch with the time when it was far more than a game or a pastime, but a buttress to my self-esteem, a substitute family, a cooling balm for my pain, a secret pleasure to my ear, a goad to my richest fantasies.

If baseball was his family, then the players were his siblings. He met few of them, but he tried to emulate them in the games he and his friends played at school. There, at the plate or in the field, Tony would pretend to be DiMaggio or Rizzuto or half a dozen other players, keeping up a babble of pseudo-baseballese, trying to hit like his heroes, trying to field like a Yankee.

Initially, I lacked the kind of surrogate family Tony had, and I felt that void deeply. But gradually I would turn music and theater into a kind of family.

I learned to play flute in the orchestra; I sang in the chorus; I built sets and played roles in the school dramas. For those who have never done these things, it is perhaps too flip an idea to say that fellow players in an amateur musical event or play can be "family." But for me—and for many others—playing the roles of adults, and singing the works of Bach and Brahms, put all who participated in a separate and special world. We *are* brothers and sisters in that world of performance. We love one another for the support we receive and give; we mourn the end of the event. No wonder so many actors in Hollywood fall in love with their co-stars.

Then, too, for me, there was the unconscious substitution of the audience for that precious audience of one I had experienced and loved as a boy of four and five. It took me years to understand these dynamics, but the sustenance they gave me was inestimable. Later still, I would use the work I did in film and television as a way to create a "family."

WHATEVER TENSIONS EXISTED BETWEEN TONY AND MYSELF, living with Missy during vacations meant creating an alliance with him. There was no other way to survive the day-by-day, minute-by-minute scrutiny from our grandmother. Clean clothes, hot baths, teeth brushing: all were in Missy's purview, even as we grew to the age of embarrassment and desired privacy.

My grandmother lived in the Alwyn Court, a thirteen-story building later added to the National Register of Historic Places. She had moved there after her husband's death in the early 1930s to be closer to Mother. The building had once had only a series of

floor-through apartments for very rich New Yorkers. It was rumored that the twelfth floor, where Missy had a five-room apartment, once held a fifteen-room dwelling for the Roosevelts.

The entire facade of the building, which was finished in 1909,
is covered in ornate carvings. Huge salamanders (the emblem of
Francis I, an art connoisseur and patron during the French Renais-
sance) flank flowers, faces, and other curlicues. I remember huge,
heavy glass doors, mounted in ornate cast-iron decorations, and a
doorman, Andy, a heavyset man with a large goiter on his neck
that got bigger and bigger over the years. The day elevator man
was Henry, a very kind person, to whom Dad gave $5 every
Christmas, and toward whom I felt guilty for years because I had
denied him a bite of my candy bar when he asked for it. I thought
he was kidding, but he was really very hungry. He told Missy, who
reprimanded me. With me, guilt lasts a long time.

On the twelfth floor, the elevator opened up on a hallway that
went three-quarters of the way around the floor, surrounding a
large courtyard. My grandmother's apartment, just at the left as
you got off the elevator, opened on a large foyer with a huge Italian wooden buffet that she had bought in Italy on one of the family's grand tours. A tiny closet of a kitchen lay directly ahead, but
through another doorway lay the large and light-filled living
room, painted a dainty blue. A fake fireplace centered the room.
The grand piano (which I now have) occupied one corner, while a
beautiful eighteenth-century breakfront desk took up part of a
wall. To the rear of the apartment, Tony and I had a big bright
bedroom, fronting on the sunlit avenue, with our own bathroom.
Furniture in this room was in blond Scandinavian style. Missy's
bedroom was even larger, also light blue, with a couch, bureau,
dressing table, and double bed. And, of course, her own bathroom. At the time, she paid $175 per month.

Missy lived off income from various investments left to her by her mother. She could afford a cleaning woman, a laundress, and a cook at various times during the week. The apartment was always neat and clean.

Coming home to this luxurious environment from the cold northland was pleasurable and exciting. We took baths in a huge tub, with enormous amounts of hot water pouring out of the spout, a vivid contrast to the once-a-week baths we were allowed at Hickory Ridge, with rusty water dribbling into the tub. The dinner Anna Fuchs prepared for us each time we returned from school was a classic, served with flair: roasted lamb, English muffins slathered with butter, roasted potatoes, avocado salad, and a rich coffee mousse dessert. It's safe to say my culinary tastes—limited though they were at first—developed at Missy's table.

Missy planned all our events. She fed us three meals a day, drew those hot baths, bought our clothes, sent us to bed, let us (or did not let us) listen to the radio programs that also fed us, chastised us for language and other disruptions of the moral code. She taught me to sing, accompanied me on my flute. In short, she attempted to do all that a mother and father would or should do.

But we had to pay for those luxuries by living with a woman who didn't know how to deal with two little boys—and certainly not with adolescents.

Tony called Missy the Queen of Daintiness, not because of her movements, but because she required us at all times to be polite, clean, and quiet, though not *too* quiet. If she kept her voice down, it was only to emphasize matters or to keep people from overhearing. Often I heard her say "colored people" in a whisper, though no one but Tony or I might be around to hear. But one of her grandchildren, my first cousin Lisa, was constantly chastised by Missy for being *too* quiet.

"Speak up, dear," Missy said, "you want to be heard."

Missy was always heard. She asked for, and received, what she wanted. In restaurants, she would demand that the piped-in music be lowered to inaudible; dinner rolls were to be returned to the kitchen to be heated (she never ate the soft inside, tearing it out to eat the crust only and saying that was better for us); and if food was not to her liking, it was not paid for. In our mother's household, servants had been treated well. In Missy's, they were tolerated.

Missy was quiet and calm on the surface, though this may have been nothing more than a depressive overlay. If she was angry, she didn't raise her voice, but simply looked sad and hurt. The only time I saw my grandmother do something truly joyful was when a famous racist Southern senator died. She had gone to the door to get the newspaper and discovered his death in the headlines of the *Herald Tribune*. Dancing a little jig, she said, "Mr. Bilbo died." It was out of character, and it never happened again. But it did set some of the political tone for us: both Missy and Dad were life-long liberal Democrats.

My grandmother wasn't terribly smart. And she wasn't much fun to be with. She had lots of money, gave generously to many charities, including the ACLU, and knew how to gather people around her. A violin teacher came once a month to play sonatas with her. Miss Dring came every week to give piano lessons. Others came for bridge, or for lunch. Some of her friends were intellectuals, and it has always been a puzzle for me that they put up with her imperious nature and with her lack of interest in serious books and serious discussions. Perhaps she dragged them into her net the way she had encouraged us to depend on her.

So while Missy was a difficult encounter, she was our protector and our governess. We had a certain obligation to obey, or at least to listen.

This posed a dilemma for us. For years we were directly under her aegis. It took many years before Dad began to fulfill the promise of being a full-time father. He lived at the Langdon, while Tony and I used Missy's apartment as our home when we came back from school for vacations. We were expected to report our comings and goings to her and to be back in her apartment at bedtime. I always obeyed; Tony did not. I got teased for being fanatically obedient to her wishes. But it made me feel secure to be the obedient little boy.

Dad was in the background, a superego to be wrestled with. He provided some money (allowances, for instance) when he could, took us to dinner and the theater at least three times during each vacation, and practiced intellectual and moral philosophy as we grew older. And eventually, when we were in high school, we spent our vacations in a small apartment he had rented on Seventy-ninth Street after leaving the Langdon.

In short, Missy took us under her roof; Dad provided peripatetic support.

And then there was Aunt Judy. If it weren't for her, I doubt that Tony and I would have had such broad exposure to cultures and the arts, not to mention the fun she gave us.

Judy was a unique character, with many eccentric flaws. She would shriek, "Oh, darling!" in a high-pitched voice whenever anything went wrong; she judged people only by their facial features, thought the Ford Foundation would eventually come through with a grant for some scheme of hers, and believed in ESP. She dressed in self-styled clothes, including hats that were no more than soft leather sewn in a Möbius strip circle. For some years, she wore only black and white, making her apartment mirror those colors. At other times, she surrounded herself with bright colors. We recognized how eccentric, perhaps even *nutty*, she was, and we were often embarrassed by her as only young children can be. But we enjoyed her jaunts by subway (Missy and Dad took cabs) to exotic venues like Chinatown and the Museum of Modern Art.

We also learned that she borrowed money from Dad and Missy, and never returned it. Dad described her as "artsy-fartsy." She found him uptight. Theirs was not a good role model for a sibling relationship. We also later learned that she, too, had made suicide attempts.

But despite Judy's bizarre behavior patterns, her total lack of criticism of us, her funny wardrobes, and the fact that she lived with—and took care of—her ailing mother (Anna Lukacs) all served to endear her to us.

And Judy took us to restaurants that whetted our appetites for exotica for decades. Turkish, Armenian, Japanese—all were part of Judy's wish for a broad education for us, and without her we would undoubtedly have missed out on cuisines and cultures that gave us endless pleasure in years to come.

STILL, THIS ENTIRE PERIOD IN OUR LIVES WAS, for me, dominated by Missy. Tony, however, could not give himself totally over to her will. In consequence, Missy lavished far more attention and love on me, sinking me further and further into the symbiotic relationship that would, in the end, both save me and render me far too dependent. Tony remained aloof. Perhaps he had been too damaged by having trusted one female figure—and having lost. Perhaps it was simply the personality he was born with. Whichever—or whatever—Tony did not say "I love you" nearly enough for Missy's pleasure. He did not put away his reading matter when she decreed lights-out. He did not lavish attention on her. But then, Tony did not lavish attention on anyone. He was a true loner, deep in whatever emotional or intellectual dialogues he was having with himself.

For now, however, we were at Missy's beck and call, and we became allies in a holding pattern against her potentially destructive cloying arms and heart. We played together in that large back bedroom and, only two blocks from her apartment, spent many afternoons in Central Park.

In the park, our spirits soared. We rode endlessly on its famous carousel, trying to pluck the brass ring from a stanchion; it would bring us luck, we believed. We were friends, not just brothers, fleeing to the sun. It was wonderful to be free to read and loaf and play without supervision. Until nightfall, that is, when Missy would run steaming hot water into our huge white bathtub, and we would scrape and scrub the park's dirt off our young bodies while she watched.

We made up our own rules for life. We ran to the large windows of the twelfth-floor apartment to look down on Seventh Avenue as the fire trucks from the nearby station rumbled noisily onto the block on their way to a fire. We read the same books (*Gone With the Wind*, the Hardy Boys mysteries) and listened to radio programs together, pushing the buttons that were labeled WEAF and WJZ, station names now long gone.

These were passionate hours as we huddled over the little Admiral radio next to our beds. These rapt moments listening to *Terry and the Pirates*, *Duffy's Tavern*, and *Inner Sanctum* bonded my brother and me as partners in a rare world of imagination. It's not that we were in love with these shows as shows but that we were in love with radio, with the magic it created. And the experience of listening *together*.

In the mornings, I woke early. I would turn to see if Tony was still asleep. Then, needing company, I would cough, whisper, or make other noises to awaken him. It was a practice that everyone complained about, but I never gave it up. I was too lonely when no one else was up, and it was too much fun watching Tony slowly come out of his dream state.

ON THE CUSP BETWEEN PRETEEN AND ADOLESCENT, Tony and I yearned to be free from Missy, but Dad—still eking out a living with the Society—said he could not afford to have us live with him. But could Dad not have lived a more frugal life, or gotten a higher-paying job, and had us move in with him? The question has been painful for me; for many years I have seen him as putting his own comfort and living style ahead of our needs. Clearly, he was uncomfortable with his parenting skills, but he did not need to abandon us. Tony felt otherwise. He thought that Dad had done his best.

Since we lived apart from Dad, our most intense relationship with him became, by default, the meals we took together.

The beginning of every meal for our father was a dry martini or two. He held his liquor well in those days, but the alcohol lubricated his emotions so that even the most enjoyable dinner ended in some criticism of our behavior, as he complained about our grades or our manner or the dry-cleaning bill. Sad to say, we rose to the bait in predictable fashion: Tony with carefully crafted counterarguments, I with sullen, down-turned face.

Dad would turn to me with one consistently uttered complaint: he said I had a *catastrophic outlook*, that I always perceived the world as a dangerous and threatening place. It meant that when someone got a cold, I might describe it as pneumonia. If someone said the sky was falling, I might believe it.

For me, that was not so bizarre. I had seen what the world could do to me, and I tried to predict the truth, even if it was a sour truth. I extrapolated from the past. To Dad, however, it was a constant reminder that I was not a happy child and that he had participated in that unhappiness. He would have preferred to see me as an optimist.

I once figured out that by the time I was fifteen, Tony and I had eaten meals at the same table twelve thousand times, many—unlike "normal" families—at restaurants, where we listened to Dad's criticisms, the rest with Missy, with whom we dined well but felt cramped. Despite—or rather because of—the fights with Dad, the meals we had together combined to form an even greater alliance between Tony and me. It wasn't just that we stood together against Dad's criticisms. Our sense of fulfillment from the food was a further connection between us. What we ate, and how much we ate, served as a sign of love—perhaps a *substitute* for the love that others had, in families that actually lived together.

We both reveled in the experience of eating, and whatever bad hands might have been dealt us in other regards, food—and the pleasures of cooking, eating, and sharing in its consumption—almost always brought joy to our souls. It was a critical source of the attachment we had for each other, and would be so for years and years to come.

Chapter Six

TOP: *Dad on an English saddle out West*

BOTTOM: *Two dude ranchers*

IN AUGUST 1945, at the end of the Larchmont summer, the war ended. So did the marriage. It had lasted a mere six months. I was very upset, but I seem to have been the only one. Dad and Ruth and Piri went on with their lives. Missy and Judy never spoke about the marriage. And Tony? Not a word. "Hey, these things happen," his body language seemed to indicate. I wanted a mother again.

In the summer of 1946, we hoped that Dad would spend time with us and that we wouldn't be sent away to camp or have to spend time with Missy. But with the Society taking up a lot of his time, Dad felt he couldn't get away for more than a couple of weeks. He arranged for Tony and me to spend the summer in Santa Fe, New Mexico, the first four weeks on a dude ranch. He would join us for the first two. This had the added benefit of taking him back to the dry desert air that physicians thought was the cure for TB.

The trip did not result in the bonding between all of us that he wished for, but it did give Tony and me something to share, and something to talk about for years to come.

Our destination was Rancho La Merced, run by a retired opera singer who had lost a lot of money in the 1929 crash. What he had left he had plowed into this little burned-out patch of sand south of Santa Fe, with a windmill to bring up water, five horses, four little rooms for guests, and a large adobe main house, the exterior hung with bleached cow horns. Dressed in cowboy boots and jeans, with broad-brimmed hats on our heads, we were soon riding down into dry arroyos and up onto the parched flatlands in search of rattlesnakes and working ranches.

Despite our discomfort at being with Dad every day, as he was always criticizing us for one thing or another, Tony and I had a lively time. Riding and sunshine appealed to us. There's a photo of the two "cowboys" grinning into the camera in one of the endless boxes of pictures in our garage, and one of Dad, looking quite trim and at ease on a slim horse. Is that an English saddle I see beneath him?

The rest of the summer, after Dad went back to New York, we spent at a camp in nearby Tesuque, north of Santa Fe. In the 1920s, Aunt Judy had gone out west to escape a debt she owed. She stayed with the German-American family that ran the camp and found respite with them from her financial and psychological troubles. She never forgot them, and it was she who urged Dad to take us to the little town. We had chores, and there were other campers with whom we had to interact. Dad's criticism on one point was well-taken: Tony and I didn't know how to meet and greet. We were shy, introverted, and unsure of ourselves. Upon learning that there were two teenage boys in the family, I even felt frightened that they might try to beat us up. Such was the continuing legacy of trauma at an early age.

One exciting moment occurred when the boys—who, it turned out, were friendly and enthusiastic—and Tony and I crept to the top of a hillock to observe as the five girls at the camp swam in the nude. It was my first time seeing a girl's naked body, and I was suitably impressed (though also suitably embarrassed).

BY 1947, gas rationing had been abolished. The country could breathe again. Live again. Buy cars again. And travel again. Bothered by the continued lack of contact with us, Dad decided to take a four-week drive across the country. He bought a secondhand 1940 Cadillac convertible from a man he didn't know, paid too much for it, and didn't have it looked over for defects. Then he asked a board member of the Society to help drive. Everything was a huge mistake. Irving, the board member, had no license, the car needed a lot of work, and bonding doesn't take place from the backseat of a car, to which we were relegated because Irving got carsick.

For most of the five-thousand-mile trek, it was a bizarre image: two unhappy boys, an alcoholic father, and a miserable sidekick. There was no bonding between Dad and us, but Tony and I pulled together tighter than ever. There were constant arguments between my brother and my father about how often we could stop; arguments between Dad and Irving about whether the convertible's top should be up or down; complaints about car sickness and our lack of "gratitude" for the experience we were having at our age. I remember feeling ill, lonely, sad, and frightened. I also remember the great stretches of Arizona highway, with nothing to see. Tony and I urged Dad to let the Cadillac out to its full speed, but he slavishly stayed under the speed limit.

Two very unpleasant events stand out: One was our arrival at the hotel on the rim of the Grand Canyon. Dad was elated. He had planned that day's drive so that we would come upon the great ditch just at sunset, and he had managed to do so.

Dad parked the car as close to the rim as he could, then he and Irving and I piled out and rushed to the edge. It was only when we got there that Dad noticed Tony was missing. Turning back to the car, he discovered my brother curled up in the backseat, reading.

The book was *The Amboy Dukes* or *The Grapes of Wrath* or *Gone With the Wind*, depending on whose memory is to be believed. It doesn't really matter, since the point was the same: Tony did not want to participate in Dad's game plan, he enjoyed reading more than sightseeing, and he had had enough of nature. Dad was furious. I don't remember him being as angry. He excoriated my brother, told him off in no uncertain terms, and stormed off to watch the sunset. Tony dragged himself out of the car and ambled into the hotel.

That night, for the first time, I became aware of Dad's serious drinking. At dinner he had more than a couple of bourbons and went to bed with a slight shine to his complexion. In the morning, he used a phrase I hadn't heard before—"hair of the dog that bit me"—as he pulled a flask from his suitcase and had a swallow. "Accch," he said, grimacing, as the undiluted liquor opened up his gullet.

On the way back, our passenger got off in Chicago. We went on to Pittsburgh. At first, Tony and I felt some pleasant anticipation at this idea. After all, there were few things we knew about Dad's early childhood, but Schenley High in Pittsburgh was one of them. We knew that Pittsburgh was important to him; maybe this would be fun.

The city was hot, filthy, ugly. Dad drank his way from one nostalgic spot to another. One morning in the hotel restaurant, we became totally fed up. He had shouted at us for coming down late for breakfast. He had scolded Tony for drinking milk too fast. We left him sitting at the table and went to our room. We didn't know that it was drink that often made him angry; whatever the cause, we didn't like it.

Not that Dad always expressed his displeasure by shouting. Sometimes it was the mere raising of an eyebrow, a quizzical look that set off just the tremor of alarm that something we had said or done was not to his liking. Then there was the glare—the "I don't believe what I just heard" stare—a prelude to angry words.

In addition to mere anger, there were certain phrases that carried particular weight. "How many times do I have to tell you?"
was one of them. "Well, I suppose you might as well learn to make
your own mistakes" was another. And the one I swore I would
never use on any other human being was what he said after asking
us to do something that we were not immediately prepared to do.
Raising his voice, he would say, "All right. *Don't* do it. Since you
always do the opposite of what I ask, then do the opposite of this:
Don't do it!" It was sarcasm, employed to demean us, and it
worked.

It was also frightening.

In the hotel room in Pittsburgh, Tony and I turned to each
other for comfort.

"I can't stand it," Tony said as we packed to leave the hotel that
afternoon.

"I can't, either," I admitted, throwing socks at the distant suitcase without any skill or luck. "Why doesn't he ever say anything
nice?"

"I'm not going to take it much longer, I can tell you that."
Tony's voice rose in ire.

We went on in that vein for some little time, and then—I suppose it was predictable—the door burst open and Dad appeared.
On the way back to his room, he had passed our door, heard the
imprecations; *he*, too, couldn't take it any longer.

"What the hell is wrong with you two ungrateful kids? I have
taken you on a trip that thousands of boys your age would sell
their souls for. And what do I get? Complaints, whining, back
talk!"

He slammed the door. I burst into tears.

Not long after, Dad wrote the following letter to another guest
at the dude ranch.

Dear May Rose:

The boys are back at school and I am quite lonely. The balance of our trip after we left SF was a huge success. It will furnish a conversation piece for the children until next year, when we hope to get to California.

I guess he saw things differently than we did.

There *were* occasions when Dad demonstrated the comforting and sheltering due two young boys from their remaining parent. He took us to plays and taught us about good theater. He recited poetry and incited us to use the right words when we both spoke and wrote. He taught us how to fold a jacket when we were packing, informed us about civil rights and civil liberties. He showed me how to carry a martini glass without spilling a drop. He trained us to match ties and shirts to socks, how to polish shoes. He tried to set us straight on what we owed the world and what, if anything, the world owed us. He had a moral sense in him that was very important, and he wanted it to be important to us. And though he lectured us on not being too individualistic or straying from received wisdom, by example he taught us to think for ourselves and search for our own truths.

These are no small matters.

IN THE SUMMERS OF 1948 AND 1949, Dad rented a small cottage on sandy soil near Peconic Bay on the then-unfashionable North Shore of Long Island. For a month and a half, Tony and I spent weeks there alone; Dad came out on the weekends. I was the chief cook and bottle washer. I liked feeding people, but I resented doing the household work—being *expected* to do it. That first summer we were fifteen and thirteen.

Dad chose this particular part of Long Island because a man

named Robert Joffe and his wife, Jessica, had a house nearby. Joffe—a radio producer who used the professional name Robert Maxwell to avoid telegraphing the fact that he was Jewish—had taken a great liking to my father and was preparing a program with him called *Criminal Casebook* in which Dad interviewed ex-convicts and got them to tell about their childhood.

Maxwell lived in Cutchogue on weekends, on an island reached by a long causeway. To the left was Peconic Bay, an offshoot of Long Island Sound. The beach here was lapped very gently by the bay's waves, and we could walk far out without losing our footing. It was sparsely populated; except for the occasional jellyfish, it was also safe. To the right of the causeway was a saltwater inlet. Here, when Joffe-Maxwell loaned us his rowboat and Evinrude outboard motor, we would go crabbing, pulling gently on a string baited with chicken to lure the unsuspecting crab up from the mud so we could net him. Patience was needed. We caught very few crabs.

Maxwell was the father I thought I wanted to have: the outgoing, swearing, gregarious, daring, generous man, the one who never criticized us, but instead offered us views of an adult world into which our own father had never led us. He taught us how to fire a .38 revolver, talked about condoms and farts and sex, and kidded us when we laughed at dirty jokes we didn't really understand. Jessica, at that time in her thirties, was beautiful and slim and daringly risqué. I fell instantly in love with her. The pair did not have children and would split up over that fact within ten years. For now, however, they were an exciting contrast to our own father, who was also enchanted with them—as Nick was with Gatsby—but who could not hold a candle to them when it came to giving adolescent boys a glimpse of a dizzy, glittering world.

Though they were men of different means and mores, Bob loved Dad, too. My father was a determinedly ethical lawyer whose view of the universe was that juvenile delinquency could be halted by kindness and psychological insight. Bob was a rambunctious radio producer, whose signal radio show, *Superman*, had captured the imagination of boys all over the world and who broke rules for his own aggrandizement, when necessary. They had both grown up in modest circumstances, without a college education, vowing to make something of themselves.

I think that Bob saw in Dad a passport to higher ideals—but he never attained them. Dad saw in Bob a chance to get his ideas known, and to make more money.

I might have taken more after Bob, but I didn't have an entrepreneurial spirit. Tony was a different matter: he was always going to follow in Dad's footsteps. He was a serious boy who was going to lead an ethically and professionally serious life. I remember once, for instance, in the middle of August in Cutchogue, a hurricane blew across the island, threatening boats, houses, and people. Tony and I went down to the causeway as the winds blew themselves out and discovered a man in his thirties trying to capture his small powerboat, which had broken loose from its mooring some miles away and was threatening to crash onto the shore. We waded out into the waist-high, choppy waters and helped bring it safely to rest on the sand. The man dug into his water-sodden pockets and gave each of us $5. Or at least I thought each of us received it. When I got home and was changing clothes, I pulled my bill from my pocket. Tony was aghast.

"You didn't take that, did you?"

I asked why not.

"You don't take money for helping people in a crisis," he said.

It was a firm and memorable reprimand from my big brother, and I was ashamed and embarrassed. This was not the first—or the last—time that he chose to be my ethics teacher. Underneath my shame, I was intensely angry.

Dad drove out to Cutchogue on Friday nights and was always a little sour when he arrived. Had we behaved ourselves? What did we eat when he wasn't around? Were we meeting any interesting kids? Did we thank Bob and Jessica for the bicycles, access to their rowboat, their Deepfreeze, their love and kindness?

These were not idle questions; Dad had strong ideas about what two young teenagers *should* be doing with their vacation. They should be learning social skills, dating girls, reading good books, and behaving themselves.

Whatever we did, it was not in line with Dad's hopes. We did *not* try to meet and make new friends. We did *not* read edifying literature. We did *not* tidy our beds. Those months were luxurious, because never again would Tony and I have so much time to ourselves with no obligations. They were also painful, because these were supposed to be the summers when Dad took the time to really *be* with us, but this didn't happen. The old arguments cropped up, and Dad's two days at the beach were always shadowed by what he thought he owed us and what he knew he couldn't give us.

What had we done in any particular week? We had probably arisen late, eaten a leisurely breakfast, packed a lunch of Kool-Aid, peanut butter sandwiches, and cookies, ridden our bikes a mile to that causeway, and sunned ourselves on the very fine stretch of sand. When the sun got too hot, we waded out into the bay, which, at low tide, provided a magnificent bed of huge hardshell clams for the picking.

We were shy teenagers, ill matched in intellect and interests: Tony was still a baseball fanatic, I liked to sail; he read history books, I chose fantasies; Tony got As at school, I was still "not living up" to my potential. But almost nothing could defeat the joy we shared when we waded out into the warm waters of the bay and pulled those clams—fully three inches across—from the sand just under our feet, filling floating plastic buckets with enough of the mollusks to make a feast for ourselves.

Unlike modern-day adolescents, Tony and I were sufficiently repressed that we avoided discussing dating or girls or sex. I learned what I knew (and it wasn't much) from dormitory discussions; what Tony knew or where he learned it, I don't know. Once he asked Dad what masturbation was (the answer from our father: "Manipulation of the penis until it gives you a pleasant feeling. It ruins things for later on"), but that was the extent of our joint sessions with Dad on sex. In fact, I didn't even think that Tony *had* anything like carnal desire. His intellectual conflagrations burned so brightly that I assumed they extinguished anything else. Later, when I realized how eagerly Tony sought out women for companionship and sex, I found out that he was just like other boys in that regard.

One crucial day in 1949 was the demarcation for me between a fearful childhood and a fearful adolescence. I had always hidden my deep fears of Dad *from* Dad: my belief that he was powerful enough to deprive me of Mother; that he had a *choice* as to whether to make our childhood safe or not; that he might wreak physical havoc on me if I told him how angry I was about losing my mother and my home.

That particular Saturday in July, my mask would come off.

It started quite simply enough with Dad asking us what we had done, and why we hadn't swept the sand out of the cottage, and why the dishes were dirty, and why this and why that. I was silent. Tony started to argue with our father. I begged him to stop, and then began to cry. My father stared in amazement. What was wrong with me?

"He's afraid of you," said my brother, revealing the dirty little secret for the first time.

Dad appeared astonished. "Afraid? Why?"

I realized that he actually had *no* understanding of the emotions I had been experiencing since Mother's death. He didn't know that I loved him and hated him, or that I feared him for what he had done to us. He didn't know that I felt guilty for having been angry at Mother when she didn't show up to say good-bye. He didn't know that part of me believed that *he* had spirited her away. And I myself didn't know that my longing for my mother had caused me such great anger and self-loathing.

The magical thinking of childhood had perverted my reasoning into two choices: either I had been responsible for my mother's death or *he* had. Either way, it caused anxiety, anger, and guilt.

If *he* was responsible for Mother's death, I was furious at him, but afraid of his power. If *I* was responsible for her death, he was going to kill me for that.

He sat there, stunned, at my tears.

"You don't ever have to be afraid of me," he said. "There's nothing I would ever do to hurt you." I didn't answer.

"Don't you know that no matter what you did, I would always love you?"

He had said this many times, and all it did was reinforce my childish belief that I *had* done something wrong.

He shrugged his shoulders in helpless confusion. The conversation ended, but the effects lingered on and on.

IN THE SUMMER OF 1951, Dad paid for Tony to go to England, as a high school graduation gift. I went off to be a counselor at a summer camp for underprivileged kids.

The camp was the wrong place for me. I had no experience dealing with young children, much less those who couldn't hear or had been through hard knocks. Despite my eagerness to do what was asked of me, despite comments about what a competent young man I was, I became frightened by what I saw as my incompetence.

I wrote to Dad:

I'm being driven literally to a mental frustration which it will be difficult for me to come out of. I know that sounds dramatic, but I am rather young to be a counselor of such 11 year olds.

But the real event of the summer occurred when I found myself in a railroad station with Dad at the end of the summer, waiting to take a train to Marblehead for a mini-vacation with Missy, where I could swim and sail and be sybaritic.

While we waited, I told him about a letter I had received from a girlfriend. In it she let me know that she was not interested in seeing me anymore. I told Dad I was very upset.

"She looks like your mother, you know," Dad said.

"Nah," I said.

"Sure," he replied, pulling out his wallet and showing me a tiny color photo of Mother, a picture I had not known even existed. I wondered how many times he had extracted that photograph from its hiding place and looked at it—longingly or angrily or with despair. I had never known what feelings he had about her, because he never talked about them. In the ten years since Mother's death, he had never volunteered a word about the woman he had married, the woman who had given birth to me. I always assumed he had been hopelessly in love, and equally hopelessly in pain when she died, but he never said. Dad never volunteered to expand on the story.

In a minute, he was about to.

I looked at the picture of my mother without having feelings about her as my mother. I was simply comparing her with my girlfriend, looking at resemblances, not thinking of Mother as a *person*, not even a dead person. At that moment I felt a greater pang at my girlfriend's negative message than at Mother's absence.

"You know that she killed herself, don't you?" Dad said, and all thoughts of my girlfriend disappeared. Had he really said that? Was I being tested for some reason? Was it a horrible joke? No, he was serious, as he'd been ten years earlier, at another railroad station, when Tony and I returned from camp.

I managed a strangled "Why?"

"She was sick," Dad said.

"Of what?"

"Mentally."

In the years since then, I've asked myself many times why I didn't take a later train, why I didn't stay and pepper him with questions. How—after all these years of unanswered and strangled doubts—could I just sit there, in shock? Perhaps it was because Dad himself was apparently unmoved, tearless. Why was he cruelly telling me the most important fact of my life at this time, when there was no room for discussion and with people milling about? No room to digest the news. Shock and awe silenced me.

Barely able to get the question out, I asked, "Why didn't you tell me before?"

"I thought you already knew."

I should have done more than shake my head. I should have shouted at him in anger. Or broken into sobs. How dare he think I knew and still never talk to me about Mother's death!

Now I understand. Now I know that he was in a permanent shock, one from which he never recovered. His own anger, guilt, sadness, and longing were never worked out—not in therapy, not in grief, not in personal conversations. He buried all of those too deep in himself to be able to communicate with his sons. Gin and bourbon became his only therapists.

I asked one more question before I left.

"Was Mother there when I was a child?"

"Physically, yes," Dad said.

I stumbled on board the train and sat in thought for the three hours it took me to get to Marblehead.

Stunned is what I felt—stunned and startled and hurt. I was furious at Mother. She had taken her own life and abandoned me in the process. I was furious at all the adults who had done nothing to protect me, to prevent her death, all those who had not told me the truth.

What was I to do with this news? I knew nothing about suicide. I had never known anyone or heard of anyone who killed himself. I felt guilty that I was angry, but equally furious that I was not permitted to shout and storm and tear my clothes.

My next impulse was that there was more to the story than the little I now knew. Dad had *done* something to make her kill herself. He had sent her away to Tripp Lake, rejected her. He had mistreated her. Because I didn't understand that Mother had a disease, a mental disorder, I concluded that Dad had been culpable. That's why he was secretive. He was *more* dangerous than I had thought!

Exhausted, I fell asleep. I couldn't think about this now. Later. Tomorrow.

I did not throw myself at Missy and ask her about Mother's death. That would have been too difficult, too soon after the ugly news. The next day, however, after four hours of cruising in a brisk wind by myself in a 110 sailboat, I felt ready to broach the subject with my grandmother. She immediately broke into tears.

"I wanted to tell you, darling. All these years. But your father . . ."

Had she really wanted to tell me? In the ten years since 1941, she had never brought the subject up, except in the most general terms. She never came close to hinting how Mother had died. If she talked about her at all, it was with tears and sobs, but she never got beyond them—to the truth.

I spoke with Dad about Mother's suicide only once more. It was the summer after I graduated from college. "You're better off," he assured me, talking about a passionate love affair (my first real sex) that had ended a few weeks earlier, "if your girlfriend was as nutty as you say."

"Would you have been better off not marrying Mother?" I asked, more as a retort than expecting a real answer. Without a moment's hesitation, he nodded his head.

"Yes. I would have been better off."

I was shocked, and hurt. Not to have had my mother at all— that was unthinkable.

In the time since I had first learned about Mother's suicide, I had given some thought to what it was like for Dad to live with her. I had talked with Uncle Ira about it, and he had given me some hint of the wild swings that governed Mother's life, of the terrible nights she must have put Dad through. That was when Ira told me that he, too, was bipolar, and I learned that he used medication to control his mood swings, medication that hadn't been available to Mother in the early 1940s. We even briefly day-dreamed together what might have been had Mother had lithium and other modern drugs instead of having to rely on shock therapy and psychoanalysis.

When Tony came back from England, I immediately told him about the suicide. He sat for a moment, but asked me no questions except "Are you sure?"

In fact, for the rest of his life, Tony showed no journalistic curiosity about his past, none of the fire and passion that he exhibited about other people's problems, their day-to-day lives. We *both* continued in psychological and intellectual denial.

Chapter Seven

TOP: *Tony, Harvard junior, 1954*

BOTTOM: *Kit, Swarthmore senior, 1956*

MORE AND MORE, Tony and I ventured out into the city without Dad or Missy in tow. Our independence from them resulted in a special brand of camaraderie, one in which Tony's greater pluck overcame my more timid nature. We explored precincts in which Dad and Missy wouldn't be caught dead—places like the seedy and precarious Hubert's Flea Circus. This inelegant emporium lay in the middle of Forty-second Street, between theaters showing endless Marx Brothers' films and flashy burlesque shows. We went there with some fear for our safety: Forty-second Street was then an area known by all to be the province of perverts, prostitutes, and pickpockets. As we walked carefully off Broadway, where brilliant billboards lit up the city, we scanned the streets for danger.

It was worth it. At Hubert's, for a few cents, we would gape at the bearded lady, the midget twins, and other oddities of the era. We would revel in frivolity. At the end, for a few extra pennies, we could peek into the flea circus itself, where we were persuaded that the little insects actually wore costumes and did acrobatics. We were gullible and easily entertained and thrilled with having witnessed the forbidden together.

Then there was *magic*. We had both decided that we wanted to be magicians. We *had* to be magicians. Under the old elevated tracks that still ran along Sixth Avenue, Tony and I visited cranky little shops that catered to amateurs and professionals alike. Above our heads, we could hear and feel the wobbly trains of the IND line as they cast shadows down onto the seamy shops below.

We entered stores filled with mystery, wishing to become midget Houdinis. We learned to do a few card tricks, to make silk handkerchiefs appear and disappear, and to watch other customers create much greater illusions. At the time, I dearly wished I could learn enough to make Mother reappear. But even Houdini couldn't do that.

SOME EXPERIENCES weren't quite so exhilarating. One December—we were no more than eleven and nine—Tony and I sauntered into a store to buy soap or sachets or some such holiday gift for Missy. Dressed up in three-quarter-length winter coats with fake fur collars, we must have looked the quintessence of little rich boys. As we walked through a quiet part of the store on an upper floor, four boys, a little older than we, approached. One asked if we knew the time. When Tony pulled back his sleeve to look at his wristwatch, the kids knew they had a good target. "Give us what you've got," the toughest said. I remember literally shivering in fright. Tony tried to face them down, while I begged him to give them something. Seeing how frightened I was, he relented. They got away with no more than $1.60, but Tony was furious with me for being such a coward. Still, I was relieved to get away without a beating, and felt secure in the knowledge that I had a big brother who would protect me.

The truest shared passion—our own little piece of heaven on earth—was theater. This was mostly an outgrowth of our early experience with Mother in White Plains, playing out our feelings on the window seat in our dining room. Being rewarded with her smile and applause.

Dad, too, found the lure of theater irresistible. I remember sitting in the living room of his small apartment on Seventy-ninth Street as he recited a peroration from *Henry V*, his hand and index finger stabbing the air, one eyebrow raised in an expression of melodramatic exhortation. It was a stirring if over-the-top rendition. Tony and I found it thrilling to hear our father perform something in a realm that we ourselves found fascinating. There were a few other recitations: something from Blake. But *Henry V* was the topper.

Once more unto the breach, dear friends . . .

There were also visits to New York theaters under Dad's tutelage—when we were at an age to appreciate the works. In those days—the 1940s and '50s—you could buy a good seat in a Broadway theater for $3.75 or $4.50. At least two or three times during our vacations, starting when we were no more than eight and ten, Dad would find the money and the time to take us to performances. These were sometimes musicals (I enjoyed watching *Finian's Rainbow* from a front-row seat), but often dramas of significant weight (*Hamlet*, *The Winslow Boy*, and others of the time). Tony and I thrilled to these experiences, and my brother would hoard Playbills in the bookcase that Missy allotted to each of us.

At Putney, we both served on stage crew; we acted in a variety of plays. Tony played Hotspur in *Henry IV*.

Together, Tony and I crammed as many performances as we could into our short vacations, discussing the assets and debits of each one, keeping the experience locked tight in our memories. We went to the Fourth Street Theater to see almost the entire oeuvre of Chekhov, played by some of the old master actors of classical theater in New York.

For these hours, we set aside sibling rivalry, the arguments, petty jealousies, angry wrestling, and fistfights. We doused our anxieties, adolescent doubts, anger, and pain in the art and craft of theater. Through theater, we were bound by an aesthetic that was built into us—by genetics, by education, by emotion. We were no longer on divergent tracks that characterized every other sphere of our lives, but focused on one agreed passion, compounded by our need for applause, our love of words, and our common blood.

Theater was also a way for both of us to use emotions that we could not—or preferred not to—express in other ways. Such feelings as anger, sorrow, and revenge could serve us well in roles that Shakespeare wrote. In real life, their expression was dangerous.

One example: In my first year at Putney, Tony and I fought, both verbally and physically, often bitterly, violently. I remember a slug match that had us rolling around the floor. Though Tony was at least ten pounds heavier than I, there was something of the desperate scrapper about me. I could hang on with my nails or teeth or legs while being pummeled. I could take the pain of punches in the hope of turning the tables on Tony. On this particular occasion, I recall being on top of him, pounding his chest, and screaming, "I'll gouge your eyes out!" It sounds almost Victorian, but those are the actual words I used.

From Putney, Tony went to Harvard. That institution was the perfect place for him. Within a few days of arriving, he had settled into Harvard Yard, where thousands of students before him, from the seventeenth century onward, had lived and eaten. He was a Lowell House resident, an intellectual in the company of like-minded individuals. He signed up for courses in religion, history, and political science. And, shortly, he set his sights on the daily university newspaper, the *Harvard Crimson*, whose membership claimed the best and the brightest, generation after generation. He hoped—no, he was *certain*—that the *Crimson* would be a stepping-stone to the *New York Times*.

Tony learned about the *Times* (and journalism in general) from a genial man named Richard Strouse, whom he encountered in the mid-1940s at Christmas parties given by friends of Dad's in Mamaroneck, the ones we attended because we didn't really think of ourselves as Jewish.

It was here that Tony, only about fourteen, once expressed to our hosts his desire to be a newspaper reporter. Dad's friend suggested he talk with Strouse, who was then at the *Times*. The older man was delighted to sound Tony out about his ideas for a future, and they struck up a once-a-year friendship in which Dick gave Tony hints about preparing for such a career. If Tony had not seen the *Times* as his primary place of employment before this point, there is no doubt that he did so after several years with Strouse at the Mamaroneck house.

Early on, Dad and I began to receive clippings from the *Crimson* in the few letters Tony sent that first year: interviews with Adlai Stevenson for his first run at the presidency and with McGeorge Bundy, then dean of the college (later architect, with John F. Kennedy, of the beginnings of the Vietnam debacle). Tony had found his calling. If he hadn't been such a good student—so adept at reading and retaining huge amounts of material—I doubt that he could have carried both his academic load and the demands of the *Crimson*. He was prodigious in his duties at the paper. He spent every evening there, and much of each afternoon. He became assistant managing editor; he wrote stories that made the front page time and again; he learned the techniques that would put him in good stead later: how to interview, how to ask questions, how to sniff out the story.

Tony was convinced that the *Crimson* would offer him the kind of training and experience necessary for an entry into the "real" world of newspaper publishing, but it always seemed to me that the *Crimson*—a daily of considerable heft—already *was* real-world publishing. At Harvard, Tony was a bylined reporter for a respected paper, one that broke stories to be picked up by other local Boston papers, one that stepped on toes that needed to be stepped on. He seemed well beyond basic training when he graduated.

No better statement of how Tony operated at Harvard could be found than in the words of another Crimsonite, David Halberstam:

> It was the fall of 1951 and we were freshman candidates for the *Crimson*. He walked into that newsroom different from the rest of us, already fully formed intellectually: he was passionately serious, yet surprisingly gentle for someone so fiercely ambitious, and finally, he was also darkly brooding . . .
>
> In the 1950s, in the world of the *Crimson*, boys taught boys. Tony was my first great mentor. He helped teach me that journalism was not just the collection of bylines, but that it had to be about something larger . . .
>
> I still take pride from the fact that the first issue our board put out in February 1954 contained a long, detailed magazine piece by Tony about the life of Wendell Furry, an associate professor of physics at Harvard and an early Communist Party member then very much under attack from McCarthy. The piece detailed why Furry had joined the party and what party meetings had been like. It was an astonishing piece of reporting. He was all of 20 at the time. The Associated Press moved the entire piece on its wire. The next day the managing editor of the St. Louis *Post-Dispatch* called to offer him a job. "Would it be all right if I just

came for the summer instead?" he said. Why just the summer? asked the editor, slightly annoyed. "Well, I still have a year of college left," he answered.

In their junior year, Halberstam was elected managing editor of the paper. Tony never got that appointment, not even as a senior.

THE YEAR AFTER Tony entered Harvard, I got into Swarthmore. Tony had told me there was no point in my even applying there because I wouldn't get in. And if I did, I wouldn't be up to the intellectual standards.

When I look back these many years, from Tony's point of view—from what he'd seen of my academic achievements so far—he was right. I *didn't* have the intellectual chops to make it. But Swarthmore deans thought otherwise. They looked at my SATs and at my nonacademic work (flute, chorus, theater) and decided they could take a chance on me.

Gradually, I found subjects in which I could both operate and write. I discovered how our professors wanted us to think about the world—broadly, deeply, with skepticism, but not cynicism. At the end of my sophomore year, I had decided on psychology as a major.

I was in the Honors Program. Seminars were small—six to eight students at most—and we were all expected to contribute both verbally and on paper. It was grueling, full of stress, but it also gave me a rigorous start to life in the real world, where independence of thought was required for the professions I eventually entered. I learned how to communicate on paper as well as with the spoken word. I came to think better of myself, academically. And, because the community was a small one (only nine hundred students), other teachers and other students knew of my work and my accomplishments. God knows how I would have fared at a large university like Harvard! I didn't give it a thought.

If I did better and better academically, my social life (a euphemism for sex and love) was dismal.

That I could not find even a temporary mate was unpleasant at the least, and often caused me abject self-doubts.

More than doubts, there was emotional and physical pain: psychosomatic stomach cramps. In my senior year, this symptom showed up whenever I had even a casual relationship with a woman. By the winter of that year, I would often have to dash to a nearby bathroom, leaving my date sitting in her seat at the movie theater or at dinner or on the front porch of the main building, alone and disgruntled. Even before this embarrassing and uncomfortable disorder sprang up, I was baffled that I couldn't find anyone whom I could love, or who would love me.

Despite my disasters when it came to romance, I was able to claim a little piece of glory at Swarthmore. Graduating with high honors and selected for Phi Beta Kappa by the faculty, I could also look back on successes in dramatic productions, a series of musical endeavors that brought me some note, and a bunch of good friends who might think me a little strange but who honored strangeness as a badge of character.

And I could look back on one of the few times I got an encomium from Tony. I had finished my junior year in the Honors Program with high grades, and Tony wrote me a letter that started off, "I'm very proud of you." This was trebly sweet. Tony had often criticized me for rushing through papers and other school exercises, for not "thinking through" knotty problems, and for being a politically naive lightweight. Few words of praise had come my way from him.

This letter, with its opening line, moved and rewarded me deeply.

At Harvard, Tony had concentrated on studying history and political science and on honing his command of the English language. His two role models were A. J. Liebling of the *New Yorker* and H. L. Mencken, who had been a star reporter and editor in Baltimore. Both men were renowned for their acerbic writing and their gourmand tastes. Mencken made outsize attacks on the establishment, while Liebling wrote exquisitely about the seamier sides of life, both here and abroad. It's hard to know which of these qualities Tony most admired. Perhaps it was Liebling's attachment to good eating and Mencken's years in Baltimore; perhaps it was their willingness to take on sacred cows.

One summer Tony worked for a Long Island newspaper, writing obituaries. I remember discussing with him the fact that the paper didn't allow anyone to use the word "cancer" as a cause of death.

It soon became clear to the family that Tony's goal was to be not simply a reporter on the *Times* but a crack foreign correspondent. He had read the work of the best of the travel jockeys who reported from distant lands. He had read James "Scotty" Reston and A. M. Rosenthal's reportage in the *Times*. He wanted to be like them. Dad scoffed at his dream, suggesting that "wishing won't make it so" and telling him not to be a creator of impossible fantasies. I don't know if Dad was egging him on or had a sincere doubt that anyone in our family could ever become that competent, that well-known.

If it was the latter, he was sadly mistaken about Tony, underestimating both the dreamer and his competence.

Chapter Eight

The draftee and Dad, Fort Benning, 1956

AFTER GRADUATION, Tony went to the Free University of Berlin to study political science. It was there that he wrote the first of a collection of about forty-five letters to me. They are remarkable for their length—he made up in pages for the months and months between epistles—and for their lack of detail about the places he was visiting. Most of the time they told about his feelings: his loneliness, anger, jealousy. Occasionally he spoke of advancement or lack of advancement. Every now and then, something of his actual life in the foreign clime came out.

The *Crimson* had trained him well. He edited his typewritten letters as if they were to be published, with carets used to insert careful changes. His handwriting was a little adolescent, but easy to read; even now, I can see it in my mind's eye, thick blue ink scrolling the letters. In some way, even though I, too, typed all my letters, it was the inked-in words that seemed the most personal to me: here is the real me, they seemed to say, beneath the smart words and the research and analysis. Here is the real Tony Lukas.

I looked forward to all his letters. I was profoundly grateful that he chose to share his experiences and his inner thoughts with me. Dad complained that he never heard from Tony, but I accepted his sporadic writing habits as part of who he was. If I didn't hear from him for months, I did not interpret this as a signal of something gone wrong, or as a sign that Tony had stopped loving me. In this regard, I let Tony be Tony.

Perhaps I should have paid more attention to the long hiatuses, spelling out—as they did—his emotional lows.

In 1950 Dad had quit the Society and became chief legal counsel to the American Jewish Committee (AJC), where he would serve a variety of constituencies, including African-Americans during the upcoming civil rights revolution. Tony and I were startled to hear that Dad was joining a "Jewish organization" because of his strong antipathy to religion. But when he pointed out that the AJC's primary role was human rights and civil liberties, we could see that the job fit Dad's experience and persona.

The main exchange of letters between Tony and myself began in October 1956. Tony had come back from Germany and was preparing to go into the army. After his deferment year, the draft had caught up with him.

I was destined for the University of California at Berkeley, where my Swarthmore mentor thought I belonged. It was the seat of some of the best research work in the country. I had also applied to Boston University's school of theater. My heart yearned in that direction. Dad, as one might expect, was all for the Ph.D. program and against the idea of his son becoming a theater director. At the time this puzzled me. It was he who had introduced us to the world of theater, he who had married an actress, he whose dramatic flair showed itself in the courtroom. What could he possibly have against theater?

In retrospect, however, the choice made eminent sense—for him. He had been disappointed by the theater: in his view, it had been at least partly responsible for stealing his wife from him. And he already thought I was too dramatic in my everyday behavior for my own good.

Of course, there was that other thing: like many a parent who had come through America's Depression, he wanted to make sure I had something "to fall back on."

Sensible, perhaps. It didn't work out the way either of us expected it to.

One letter I received in Berkeley spelled out that Tony was suffering both from a cold and from the fact that the next day he would have to appear at the army for his physical. He was not upbeat about his next two years, but he did say that he would be more sanguine if he could get into the psychological warfare division of the army or perhaps work on *Stars and Stripes*, the famous army newspaper.

By mid-November, he was at Fort Benning in basic training. He moans about having to get up for KP duty at three-thirty in the morning and explains how he and two law school grads found that by standing in the middle of formation, they didn't get lopped off for kitchen duty: peeling spuds. The close-order drills, the early formations, the strict adherence to schedule, and the fear of being sent into combat in the Korean War provided him with plenty of worries and complaints.

He talks about my "condition," his coy word for my intestinal problems. They had continued unabated after college, and endless tests proved they were clearly *not* physiological in origin. I had begun psychotherapy to try to get to the bottom of them, but this proved more difficult than anyone had supposed. I still had to decide where I was going and with whom based solely on the nearby availability of a bathroom.

If it hadn't been for the miracle of paregoric (an opium derivative prescribed by my doctor) and the companionship of good male friends who understood my dilemma, I might have become more agoraphobic than I did. As it was, I was afraid to venture too far outside the dorm and, for a while, seldom dated.

I don't think Tony ever really bought into the concept that a psychological problem could turn into a physical one. Psychology was not among the courses he took at Harvard, and he was ignorant of Freudian concepts. Though the idea of psychosomatic ailments had been around for decades, he knew little or nothing about them. In this letter, he suggested I not be "too *clinical*" about my problem. "I try to take these things in stride," he said.

I don't know what he meant by "these things," but his lack of understanding at that time was very upsetting. I felt crippled by both the physical and the psychological characteristics of my intestinal disorder—for that is precisely what it was—and his statement made me angry. How could he know what I was going through if he'd never had a problem like this? Why did people think it was just an upset stomach when I had done all the medical tests and knew that I had something that Maalox and Pepto-Bismol weren't going to cure? Something alien and disconcerting and frightening had happened to me, and Tony's lack of understanding disturbed me deeply.

I didn't hear from him again until March 1957. He was finishing up his basic training at Fort Benning and studying how to write propaganda to be beamed into Korea. He sent mock army forms that "excused" him for forgetting my birthday.

The same week, in my apartment in Berkeley, I received a telegram from Dad saying that he and Betty Field had been married. Betty had some reputation as an actress: her role in the film *Of Mice and Men*, as well as numerous Broadway plays, confirms her talent. The fact that her name was Elizabeth, and that she was an actress, speaks volumes to me about Dad's inability to let go of Mother.

Tony had attended the wedding, and I was upset. No one had alerted me, or given me the chance to say I wanted to be there. I had met Betty a number of times but had no feeling one way or the other about her. By this time, another mother was not something I sought. Betty had three teenage children from a previous marriage. Given the difficulty Dad had with raising us, Tony and I wondered how he would deal with them.

In April, on his way to Japan for active duty as a psywar specialist, Tony visited me in California. I showed him around the campus and told him that I was not happy with the psychology department at Berkeley and didn't think I'd continue graduate studies beyond May. At Berkeley everyone seemed interested only in passing Ph.D. exams, not in the subject matter itself. What had impressed me at Swarthmore was the passion for the subject, but that was completely missing from my experience at Berkeley. I found myself more and more drawn back to the theater—to stagecraft and acting. I joined the Mask and Dagger Society, a student performance group. I began performing in their musical revues. Once again, I had found a substitute family.

Tony and I took a grand tour of the area, driving north, then stopped in the elite little bayside town of Sausalito to take lunch at Sally Rand's, a waterside bistro run by the former fan dancer. I remember a delicious chilled Beaulieu Vineyard Pinot Blanc, oysters, and shrimp.

Conversation at the restaurant roamed from my studies in psychology to Tony's dread of going to Tokyo for the army. As the wine streamed through our veins, we shared memories of past meals and warmed to each other in a way that had seldom been true during our adolescence. Perhaps, I thought, we are going to be comrades after all.

A little later, Tony let me know that my recent change of heart about my career worried him. "Don't jump. You may come to regret it," he cautioned. I wrote my father:

> *You are probably afraid that I am romanticizing (to use your phrase) the whole field of show business. Having watched Paul*

Lukas, Betty Field, Bob Maxwell, you are afraid that I feel the thrill of the business, the glamour, and the glory, without being sensible of the hard roads that must be traveled, the jobs without reward, the years without glory, and the small probability of eventual success. Sure, I'm thrilled by the big top, the lights, the makeup, the music, the elephants, the money, the gaudiness. I love applause. But I also think I have talent. You will say that I am easily discouraged by difficult enterprises; perhaps, with one disappointment, one "no" from a producer, I might give up. I'm working on that.

"Working on that" refers, I suppose, to my ongoing psychotherapy.

What startles me at fifty years' remove from this letter is how calm I was. Timid to the extreme with my father, I can *feel* myself growing emotionally in the correspondence at this time. I am willing to share my personal feelings with him. I am willing to risk his reactions. In some ways, this was similar to what Tony did with me: using letters to expose energies and emotions we could not share in person.

Soon, Tony was in the business of disinformation—broadcasting to the Chinese and the North Koreans what the Americans *wanted* them to believe. In short, after only a week in Tokyo as a psychological warfare specialist, he had decided it was okay to write propaganda, to do what his normally liberal views would never have allowed him to contemplate previously. We were both brought up to tell the truth, and in later years Tony would be horrified at anyone who justified lying, even in times of war.

Still:

I continue to write most of the commentaries every week. I've written on virtually every subject which could be of any benefit to

our propaganda line . . . from the UN report on Hungary to the
disarmament talks in London . . . I remind myself I'm not work-
ing for the Times. I'm writing for Psychological Warfare, which
is engaged in propaganda. Here, there is no such thing as objec-
tive news.

Five of the writers and performers from Mask and Dagger and
I decided to move to Los Angeles, setting up house way out in the
San Fernando Valley. I was the only one who had a job: Bob
Maxwell, Dad's old radio producer, had put me on the *Lassie* tele-
vision program staff, as dialogue coach.

It was a new world for me—television, film, Hollywood, palm
trees, celebrities, long hours on location, technical stuff I'd never
studied—and I was thrilled.

By August 1957, Tony was anything *but* thrilled. He was sick
of barracks life. He moved into a private room in someone's
house in Tokyo; it was small but pleasant. He removed his shoes
before entering and spoke of how wonderful the light and silence
were. The "only problem," he reported, was that he couldn't get
to early morning rounds of cleanup at the barracks. Was this a coy
way of saying he actually was AWOL during this mandatory
work, or did he rush to the barracks at 5:30 a.m., then return to his
apartment?

I do know that he got up one morning at 5:30 to climb Mount
Fuji for the joy and awe of sunrise. In a footnote to that letter,
Tony vowed not to "get bitter" at the army for taking two years
out of his life.

But by January 1958, he had become desperate to get out of the
army early—"at any price." He began to look for positions on gubernatorial campaigns around the United States, thinking he
might be valuable as a press aide.

He remarked on the loneliness of a writer's life and how *I* was

lucky because I was "good with people." I reflect now on this statement and feel the surprise I must have felt then. How different
one's self-image is from the perception of others. "Good with people." I didn't think so. I felt frightened at approaching strangers.
As a newcomer to a room full of people, I crept along the edges.
Everyone seemed, if not hostile, then supremely blah about my
presence. I couldn't even get up the nerve to suggest a game of tennis to a colleague, for fear of being rejected.

Just after his twenty-fifth birthday, Tony told me the long wait
was over. The army would give him early release to work on the
gubernatorial race in Massachusetts.

In June, he took a three-week leave in "the hinterlands" of
Japan, promising to bring me a silk kimono if he could get to L.A.
With the prospect both of release and of vacation, the tone of the
letter was much lighter. He bantered about my appearance in
LIFE magazine a few months before, as part of a cover story
about *Lassie*. (There was no mention of the fact that by then I'd
been laid off from the show because the producer's wife wanted to
do my job herself!)

I struggled to find work in the television industry, using the
few contacts I had made. I wrote outlines for shows, submitted
them, and counted the rejection letters.

In Boston, where he settled after the army, Tony was making
strides. He had found "a terrific girl and apartment," as well as a
job on a political campaign, but added, "I'm more alive and more
depressed than in years."

This statement reveals a great deal about Tony. He is "alive"
because he sees possibilities in this political work to catapult him
onto a newspaper like the *Washington Post* or the *Christian Science
Monitor* or maybe even the *Baltimore Sun*. But because he isn't
there yet, he finds this a depressing time. So much to hope for, but

so much unsettled. And so much impatience. He ends, "Maybe I'll have to go back to the *Post-Dispatch*," the same newspaper that was so impressed by Tony that it offered him a permanent job during his junior year at Harvard, but was now too low a prize for him to contemplate.

In the meantime, I had entered a serious regime of psychoanalysis. My physical symptoms had not diminished, even though the paregoric worked most of the time. And my depression kept getting worse, especially when I contemplated continuing to live way out in the valley, subsisting on unemployment benefits, and seeing nothing coming my way.

Soon, Tony wrote that he had again been depressed, "very depressed," and attributed it to his inability to get a rise out of any major newspaper.

I DON'T KNOW when I stopped thinking of the word "depressed" as a general description of sadness or disappointment and started thinking of it clinically. Or when I realized it was a medical term that applied to Tony—and to me. When he wrote that letter in 1958, Tony was not suggesting that he had a mental disorder. In fact, I'm not sure that he *ever* thought so. "Depressed" and "depression" were figures of speech, more like "sad" or "disappointed."

I should have known better. Not only had I studied psychology and knew the distinction between sadness and depression, but I was all too aware of my own mental instability. Since the fall of 1955, my senior year of college, I surely *knew* what depression was and what it could do to the body and the mind.

Due to my current analysis I was knowledgeable enough to realize that what had been labeled "neurasthenia" was more likely a combination of an anxiety disorder, psychogenic stomach disorder, and dysthymia—or cyclical depression. I was confident that psychotherapy would work. I just had to enter into it full throttle.

When Tony wrote that he was "depressed," however, I wasn't connecting the dots. I thought I was the only one in the family who had serious psychological problems—serious enough to inhibit my career path, my social life, and my sense of enjoyment, though not so serious as to require close supervision or to keep me from occasional moments of pleasure. In short, I was like millions of Americans—troubled but not mentally ill.

I figured Tony was just looking for his place in the world after the army, and that takes time and effort. Of course he'll be unhappy from time to time, I thought, but he's strong.

In late 1958, from the heavens came a bid from the Baltimore *Sun*. Tony was thrilled because it was in a city he knew had "culture," a city where Mencken spent many productive years. With the *Sun* job, he reported, he would be up and running into the future. But he also said he was tired of dragging all over the place, tired of not having someone to love him ("I'll take the first sweet thing who comes along"), and, most important, "I'm fearful of letting anyone else know just how unsure I am of myself and my ability. I am too concerned with showing my best face, even if it means painting a false one."

Tony's lack of elation revealed a pattern that I can understand: we both could work extremely hard for our achievements, but once they were accomplished, we could equally express despair that they weren't greater or that people weren't noticing how well we were doing, weren't applauding us. For both of us, there was constant devaluation of our achievements.

Over the next year, ups and downs persisted. Tony would complain bitterly that he was on the "lobster shift," where "not enough writing will come my way." He could not understand why once again he had to undergo apprenticeship. As a twenty-six-year-old reporter who had seen service in the army, at the *Harvard Crimson*, and at two other newspapers, he was infuriated at being forced to show his mettle once again.

Later, his mood would switch. "In the past two months I've been doing more writing than I ever thought possible on a paper this size and it's all been getting in. From my contacts . . . I gather that it's been well received and that the city editor likes my style." He had gotten two bylines ("almost unheard-of for a new man"), and it's clear that the reporter Tony is to become had already begun to show itself. He even admitted that he was getting a good "education" in the basics of journalism—forgoing the hubris of his remarks only a few months earlier.

Understandably, he relates that with all this work he has no time for a social life—no dates, no girls. He has even had no time to read books. He's lonely. He wishes he could come to California to see me—we've seen each other only five days in the past four years—but he's too busy writing.

In September, I decided to join Tony back east for Missy's seventy-fifth birthday. The trip reunited Dad, Tony, and me for the first time in two or three years. It was not without its tribulation (I was fired from the trucking company I had been working for because I overstayed my leave), but it was good to hear how Tony was doing on the *Sun*, and we took the time to attend some theater together. On leaving, we promised to be in closer touch by mail.

In December, back in L.A., I got a call from Bob Maxwell, who had bought the rights to MGM's *National Velvet* to make a television series. Would I like to come along as associate producer?

Tony congratulated me, but complained, "This is the most unimaginative, dull and uncreative city desk you can imagine." He's depressed, but can't fight it off. Nothing looks right to him, not his present "woman" or the job, from which freshness and spontaneity have evaporated. He says he's looking for a position either at the *Washington Post* or the *Herald Tribune* in New York. At the end, he apologizes for his "sour note for a sour feeling."

I wonder if Tony was not simply a depressive but subject to the waves of affect that characterize bipolar disorder. If so, it might explain the intense irritability that preceded his depressive episodes and the bursts of enthusiasm that occasionally accompanied his work.

My own life—like that of anyone trying to get a break in a tough industry—had its ups and downs. While I was very active, I had terrible problems with my so-called love life. I found myself in an on-again, off-again relationship with a young architecture student that proved difficult to stay in and difficult to terminate.

I didn't know whether she loved me or never wanted to see me again. She found it difficult to articulate her feelings. During our phone calls, there were often long, unbearable silences between us. I felt adrift, uncertain about my ability to be loved, uncertain about her feelings.

My psychoanalyst kept asking me why I felt so much rejection and sorrow when this woman couldn't respond to me. Was it, perhaps, an echo of the silence of my mother? I wasn't prepared—at that time—to countenance any such Freudian interpretation.

But one thing is certain: I was not equipped to deal with a romance in which I got less than 100 percent. Sadness and anger surged through me. Why didn't this woman care for me as much as I cared for her? My psychoanalyst asked me why I had *chosen* her, suggesting that the fault might lie not with her but with my choice of potential mates. Was I perhaps picking women who *couldn't* love? Was I playing over and over again the broken record of the death of my mother? In years to come, this phantom would sabotage me.

Meanwhile, I decided I needed to get away for a while. I would take a vacation. I asked Tony to join me.

Chapter Nine

The Times *man, Mexico, 1960*

IN A LUSH GARDEN on the grounds of the María Cristina, an inexpensive colonial-era hotel in the heart of Mexico City, my brother sits and reads the *New York Times*. For years, this is how each day will start. No matter where he is, he has to read that paper. And even though he is still working for the *Sun*, he has to know what Scotty Reston is saying. Later, Susan and I made it a matter of speculation whenever Tony visited us to see how far he would travel and how long it might take to get the paper for his morning read. In Mexico, he had only to travel down to the Paseo de la Reforma, where the Hilton sold the *Times*.

While the paper was being read, everything else came to a halt. No one was allowed to interrupt; no crisis, excluding an earthquake, might shake Tony from finishing the sports and foreign desk sections. It was a ritual of enormous consequence.

Since the trip to Mexico was our first vacation together in almost ten years, I was impatient to get on to the business of pleasure. But Tony instructed me in the importance of his morning read, and I came to respect and tolerate it, no matter how long it lasted. I had borrowed a 35 mm camera to capture interesting moments on the trip—my first effort at taking still pictures—and somewhere there is a slide of Tony in his cordovan shoes, J. Press button-down shirt, and crewneck sweater from his Harvard days reading the *Times* in the María Cristina's garden on that sunny morning in May 1960. We laugh at it, my wife and I, for the absurdity of the image—all those northern clothes, that concentration on *news* in the midst of southern beauty and southern climate—but we also admire it for the image of Tony's dedication to dreams of glory.

The Mexico trip was not only the first expanse of time we spent together after adolescence but the last before I got married. As such, it had then, and has now, an aura of "golden time" about it—that important hour at the end of the day when filmmakers wait until the sun's glow is just perfect for capturing life not as it is but as we wish it to be. As a nascent photographer and wannabe in the film industry, I knew about golden time. The term would reverberate with multiple meanings for my entire life.

Originally, Tony had wanted to join me for my birthday in March, but he was working hard at the *Sun* and couldn't get away. I, on the other hand, was having my own busy time—completing the *Velvet* pilot, which seemed to take forever. Then we got the idea we could take a vacation together while Maxwell waited to hear whether the *Velvet* series would be picked up for production; Tony had accrued vacation time. Hey, we could go somewhere with each other. We decided on two and a half weeks in Mexico.

Living in Los Angeles made Mexico a perfect choice for me. It was close, the airfare was low, I loved Mexican food and Mexican music. Tony readily agreed. Mexico and its beaches seemed a wonderful option after a rough Maryland winter, and it turned out several acquaintances in Baltimore had friends or restaurants to suggest in Mexico. I started studying Spanish. I knew Tony wouldn't know a word of it, since he was resistant to the study of languages unless he was paid to do it. But I hated to travel without some knowledge of a country's language. By the time I left for Mexico City a month later, I had acquired a good working knowledge of the basic verbs and grammar. Enough, at least, to get us through our travels.

The plan was that I would fly to Mexico City on May 4, wait in our hotel for him to arrive the next day, and then we would spend two and a half weeks exploring. I used the patron saint of guidebooks—Kate Simon's *Mexico: Places and Pleasures*—to plan our holiday, but I must have missed the section on fiestas, because I arrived just before Cinco de Mayo, a day of jubilant celebration in Mexico, a fanfare for an exhilarating nineteenth-century victory over colonialism. Tony would not see it, but my memory of our trip together is forever colored by the experience of that first night. Shortly after I returned to California, I tried to convey in writing my love affair with Mexico through that first night's experience:

Fireworks. The sky was bright with pinwheels and rockets. I walked down the Avenida de la Reforma, buffeted by the celebrating crowds. Huge billboards announced the lottery. The streets were crowded with celebrants. I continually tried to assimilate the smells and sounds of this, the biggest street in Mexico City at nine o'clock in the evening of the day before the day they call Cinco de Mayo. It was a glorious cacophony. Boys, no more than six or seven years old, ran in and out of the crowd, selling *fracciones* of lottery tickets; street musicians competing with each other in friendly disharmony. Tacos, frying over charcoal, summoned the juices of thousands of stomachs; beggars, blind, one-legged, armless, plied their trade. Automobiles careened around traffic circles in unending spirals with no break for vehicles entering from side streets.

Umber, pink, terra cotta, ochre, rust—the earth tones of Latin America made the landscape a living painting. The streets were alive, crawling with millions of people: farmers in two-piece, white cotton work clothes; charros in broad-brimmed sombreros, with silver buttons down their trousers; ladies in embroidered dresses; businessmen, striding along in three-piece suits; Indian peasant women, their tattered dresses covered by rebozos, in which they carried their infants. All in an infinity of colors. Poverty, such as I had never seen before, marched side by side with luxury. Hands were held out in supplication to passing strangers who jingled in jewelry or leather boots with spurs. Above, the sky crackled: From every rooftop, amateur pyrotechnicrats set off fireworks, so that the evening sky was pink and white and green, and the air smelled of gunpowder.

A never-ending parade of festivals. I drank and ate and danced in the streets, watching the fireworks.

This was a romanticized version. I didn't actually dance and revel in the cacophony. In fact, I was frightened by the noise and the strange customs. At the age of twenty-six, I had not yet conquered my childhood fear of being alone. Sent away to camp at the age of six, learning that my mother had died, that my father would go away to a hospital, and that I, too, must go away, had left me with a host of residual anxieties that surfaced at times like this.

In adolescence, Tony and I had gone everywhere together, and I was able to bear up even when we were robbed by those toughs in Bloomingdale's *because* Tony was with me. But when I was alone, even in my adult years, the fears of being abandoned and left behind in some forbidding place often came back. Tony thrived on new places; I learned how to make film and sat in the safety of an editing room. It was a striking contrast, and not until I married and traveled extensively did the fear of abandonment in foreign environments begin to leave me.

In the morning, with the sunshine, I was a new man. Refreshed, I breakfasted on huevos rancheros and strong coffee. In those days the María Cristina was already a rarity: it had enough real estate to set the pleasing hotel onto the grounds of that large garden—at a moderate cost. There was no air-conditioning, but the thick walls of the hundred-year-old building made that unnecessary. The rooms were small, but who spends time in rooms in Mexico? The restaurant served a delicious breakfast of eggs, tortillas, and fresh papaya; a little bar off the garden boasted a guitar trio that serenaded all night long. We were in paradise.

For those few days in Mexico City, Tony and I were fellow travelers on an equal footing, something that had never been true before. I had read up on the country and its offerings; I spoke Spanish. Tony was without any of the language, and he hadn't had time to learn anything of the country's history. For once, I had done the research; he had not.

We took the tourist trail recommended by Kate Simon. We ate at the restaurants she suggested—Danubio, in the downtown area, Hamburgo 76, in the Zona Rosa. We looked through the old Museum of Anthropology, where glyphs and stelae mingled with jade masks and stone images of Coatlicue—the goddess of death. History was Tony's passion, and he enjoyed this look into the pre-Columbian era.

We went to the huge square—the zocalo—where an immense cathedral stood on the former site of an Aztec temple. We stood in awe of the thousands of people crowding public streets. On the Paseo de la Reforma, we took the *peseros*, gypsy cabs that plied only that route, charging but one peso for a group ride.

We were entranced by all of it—the cuisine, the ancient myths, the artifacts. We sneezed our way through dusty hallways in search of Rivera and Orozco murals, stopped at midday to dine on *langostinos al mojo de ajo*—succulent crawfish with a crisp garlic sauce. We listened to mariachis as they serenaded lovers in raunchy Plaza Garibaldi and heard the marimbas play through the night in the Zona Rosa near our hotel.

The second night in the city, we took a cab to the Frontón

México, the country's paean to jai alai. The atmosphere inside was more like that at a prizefight or a play. Spectators sat in the dark. Players were in a brightly lit arena, separated from us by a huge rope net that hung from ceiling to floor. They slung the pelota at hundred-mile-an-hour speeds from their rattan *canastas*, white flannel pants gleaming in the luminescence. During lulls between shots or games, bookies cried their odds, and bettors in the audience caught a tennis ball into which a slit had been cut—permitting them to insert pesos, then toss it back to the tout, who remembered everyone's bet. At the end of play, which could last from a few minutes to a breathtaking half hour, one team—Rojo or Azul—had won, and winnings could be collected. Tony and I watched enthralled, but didn't wager. We couldn't understand the odds.

Three days later, we went back to the airport and flew by DC-3 to Oaxaca. It was an early morning trip, so we skipped breakfast.

This, too, was on Kate Simon's trail, though she hadn't warned of the creaky old World War II warplane that flew the route—so drafty that during the entire flight a hiss of cold air came into the cabin from a break in one of the windows. The landing in Oaxaca was bumpy; skimpy brakes sent us skidding to the very edge of the runway. We would have to take the same plane to Acapulco two days later.

As we traveled the short distance into that city of ten thousand people, to the Marques del Valle hotel, I saw for the first time what Mexico would evoke for me the rest of my life: old men with brooms made of straw, or of thin tree branches, sweeping the pathways full of bougainvillea blossoms that had fallen in perfect circles—like painted skirts around the mother vines; young girls, on hands and knees, black tresses tied up in braids behind their heads, washing endless miles of marble corridors. Later, it would also mean guitar trios on the beach in Acapulco, the blind gui-

tarists of the zocalo in Oaxaca, the sad marimbas; stelae and pyramids, standing in fields of broken stone, mute against the harsh
light. Pomegranates, dripping from the trees; police whistles like
birdcalls; women in endless poverty; mescal, tequila, and exquisite
dark sauces with sharp and subtle tastes.

We checked into our room and went immediately to the lobby
to seek Victor, a tour guide who had been recommended to me in
L.A. Victor put us in a tired car and drove to Monte Albán, the first
of the two great ruins in Oaxaca. We were tired, hungry, and dis-
combobulated by the dust and heat. Tony had spent two years in
Baltimore and seemed to be able to sweat his way through humid
days without discomfort; I found the heat unnerving. Unlike the
pyramids outside of Mexico City, no structures at these Zapotec
and Mixtec sites were above a few feet tall. And while Victor made
much of the "Greek key" motifs on the low walls, my mind kept
wandering to cool patios and a lunch of guacamole. On the way
back to Oaxaca, we stopped at a local jewelry store. Jaguars made
of onyx and jade stared out at us from the floor-to-ceiling shelves.
Next door was a bar. Victor poured us a couple of shots of mescal,
our first taste of the stuff. By the time we reached our hotel, mid-
afternoon, food was the last thing on our minds. I badly needed a
siesta.

Our room was on the ground floor. Its large, shuttered windows opened onto a square patio in the front of the hotel, shaded
by a huge cypress. Here, in the evening, marimba players would
serenade the hotel while its guests sipped rum or tequila drinks.

Tony and I drifted off to sleep. When I awoke, a few hours
later, it was dusk, and I could hear the sad strains of "Zandunga,"
a Tehuantepec song, played on marimbas in the patio. My nose was
running. I wiped it with my sleeve, but it continued to run. Opening my eyes, I saw that my shirtsleeve was covered in blood. I was

bleeding copiously. I went to the bathroom, grabbed a towel, and held it hard against my face, but the towel quickly turned deep red. I began to panic. What would happen if this bleeding didn't stop?

Waking Tony, I had the presence of mind to have him call for ice from room service. It was a long time coming. Meanwhile, I watched him for signs of fear, for Tony was frightened of physical pain or illness. If a hypodermic needle came near him, he had been known to faint. A syringe for bloodletting would make him turn his head away in nausea. Once, I was told, he even fainted during a simple eye examination. From time to time, he reported that he was suffering from one serious disease or another, even when there was no evidence.

Now, however, he just sat on his bed and watched me bleed. Perhaps it was only *his* pain and blood loss that were frightening. From time to time he would ask, "Any better?" I would check the towel, then shake my head.

Finally a slim young girl in a white dress entered the room and stood at the door, aghast at the sight of this young American stretched on the bed, holding a bloody towel to his face. Tony took the bowl of ice, the precious cargo already melting in the tropical heat, and the girl fled.

I held what was left of the ice to my nose, hoping that the bleeding would stop. Tony sat on the other bed, and we talked about what would happen if it didn't. Would he have to find a doctor? Would we fly back to the States? In my innermost thoughts, I wondered whether I would die here.

Outside, the marimbas continued to play their sad, tango-like tune about Zandunga, the ghost who haunted a man's memory:

Ay! Zandunga!
Zandunga mamá por Dios

Zandunga no seas ingrata
mamá de mi corazón . . .

Around midnight, as I drifted in and out of sleep, the bleeding finally stopped. I was hungry and persuaded Tony to phone down for toast and tea, which I thought would be good for an ailing American and his ravenous brother. Instead, a tostada—the vegetable-laden salad Mexicans serve on a tortilla smeared with refried beans—arrived. Tony ate it, and I went back to sleep.

In the morning, the marimba and its sepulchral players had gone; traffic was up to its daytime cacophony; the streets were alive—and so was I.

A few days later, the same DC-3 did take us, without incident, to the small airport at Acapulco. We found a tiny, grimy, and by no means upscale motel near the northern end of town—away from all the shiny resorts, but close to a small beach touted by a local taxi driver. We thought we would swim in the motel's pool, but it was cloaked in green slime and apparently hadn't been used for years.

On the beach, however, we found a sybaritic heaven. Strolling guitarists serenaded us for a few pesos, singing "Malagueña," "Crei," "Cuando Caliente el Sol," and other laments of the South. Shrimps and oysters could be purchased from our beach chairs for mere pennies. The sun was hot and magical, and though we shaded ourselves as much as possible from its rays, we could feel its healing power in our backs and legs.

Though we occasionally argued over how long we should stay at the beach (Tony was just hanging out; I wanted to get on with explorations), we were beginning to accept the rhythms of each other's lifestyle and compromised sufficiently to stay on good terms.

We were also both learning a lot about a new world outside of ourselves. We had not been prepared for Mexico—for its colonial apparatus, the richness of its culture, the poverty of most of its citizens, the acceptance by them of *us*, the *yanquis*.

At this point, we began to address our assumptions about the country, about our right to be there, to be waited on, to get good lodging and great food while tens of thousands went homeless and hungry. It happened in one of the first restaurants where we ate. Tony softly whistled for the waiter. I looked up, surprised. This would be considered outrageous behavior in the States. But Tony assured me that his friends in Baltimore said it was quite the custom here. And, to be sure, the waiter didn't seem bothered at all by the whistle. "*Sí, señor, mande*," he said. "What can I do for you?"

This began a discussion between us as to where we were and what we were up to. As vacationers, we made assumptions about *our* comfort, *our* safety. But what about *their* comfort and safety? At the University of Mexico, and at the museums, through the great muralists, we came face-to-face with colonialist history and its oppressive practices.

Which is not to say that we became zealots for the rights of the poor. We were still tourists in a strange land, still trying to secure *our* own comfort and safety. But we did come to understand something of what the indigenous people of this country were up against.

As we went from place to place, we gobbled it all up. This was better than history from a book: this was what the ancient Greeks called *historin*—experiencing the world, not just learning about it.

One experience came close both to bonding us and to separating us. I don't know about other siblings, but my brother and I never talked about sex. It just wasn't part of our interaction. This was partly embarrassment, partly prudishness, partly a desire for absolute privacy. Nevertheless, I was aware that Tony used prostitutes. In Mexico City one night, he disappeared into the darkness around 10:00 p.m. and told me later he had been looking for a bordello. On the one hand, this was a mystery to me—both Tony and I had women friends who, even in the Victorian 1950s and early '60s, were amenable to sex—but it also seemed natural: Didn't *all* men engage in this kind of thing? Up to this point, I had not done so, but I chalked that up to my *unnatural* shyness and morality about sex.

In doing research for our vacation, I had heard that there was a seedy backside to Acapulco: a little red-light district called Rio Rita. It was up in the hills and said to be a "must" for tourists. Tony said he wanted to see it. Would I accompany him? For me, Rio Rita was a chance to do something I'd never done before. Though it caused me a certain tremor (I had seen the raunchier districts of Mexico City, and I knew that foreigners were often robbed there), it was also something a "man" had to experience, wasn't it?

The single street that was Rio Rita was long, gaudy, brightly lit, and consisted of nothing but cantinas. It was not overrun by tourists—far from it—and unlike similar joints in other Mexican towns and cities, the interiors of these bars were clean and tidy. And quiet. There were a few tables at which a few women sat, idly swinging their legs. Tony and I picked a place to sit and asked for Dos Equis beer. Nearby sat a young woman, perhaps my age or a little younger. Despite my aversion to the idea of having paid sex, I was curious. The place seemed clean, there were no menacing figures ready to grab pesos from our wallets.

Lifting myself off the chair at our table, I took the plunge and sat down next to her. Esperanza (Hope) was her name, and she didn't speak English. My Spanish was sufficient to make a deal:

thirty pesos for a quick trip to the back room. She would have been happy to spend the night at our motel, but that didn't fit my desire or my budget.

Before Esperanza and I left for the back room, Tony spied a dark-haired woman in the far corner and asked me to interpret for him. This turn of events had not occurred to me. How was I supposed to carry this out without becoming a part of Tony's sexual life itself? It turned out I didn't need to: the woman spoke good English. I left them at our table and went into the back with Esperanza.

At the doorway to the nether regions of the cantina, she stopped and held out her hand. "Money," she said, in thickly accented English. I put thirty pesos into her hand and she disappeared. Had I just been robbed, or was she off to give the money to the management? In a few seconds, she returned, and we went to her little room.

In some ways, this was exactly what I had expected of a Mexican bordello: dim red light, a tiny bed, walls covered with dime-store folk art. In the corner was a shower.

Looking back, I still feel badly about the next fifteen minutes. Not just because I was contributing to a deleterious way of life, but because of my inability to feel anything verging on interest in this thin, only vaguely sexy young woman. I was asked to take a shower. I provided a condom from my pocket (this was before AIDS, but not before syphilis or gonorrhea).

The experience was short, sordid, and not very satisfying. But I had now practiced that male skill—going to a prostitute—and could add that to the list of things I did that others said had to be done to be a real man. I would never repeat it. For me, affection was a necessary component of sexual activity.

Tony and I never talked about this experience. The very fact that we didn't put a bit of distance between us: here was one more thing that was improper to discuss; one more *secret* that had to be kept.

ON THE NEXT-TO-LAST DAY IN ACAPULCO, Tony and I took a little boat that carried just six passengers over to La Roqueta, a tiny island about half a mile from our usual beach. The sand was cleaner, the crowd thinner, and the shade deeper under groves of palm trees. The afternoon was spent drinking beer, eating shrimp, napping in the sun, and bathing in the salty, bath-warm water. We were mindful that the last boat left at 5:30; after that hour, it was swim for it or stay the night on the island.

Toward 4:30, we noticed four or five boys in their subteens playing soccer on a wet and slippery stone terrace near a refreshment stand. Since Tony and I had been middling players in high school, we asked if we could join in.

It was a silly move, since even ten-year-old boys in Mexico were bound to be better than we. We feinted and kicked and caused a great deal of laughter. Then Tony's foot went out from under him on the wet stones. He fell on his left elbow, causing instant swelling and intense pain.

The boys were worried—for about ten seconds. Then they took off for parts unknown. Suddenly the place was quiet and dark. I looked at my watch: it was 5:15. Would we miss the boat? Tony was now sitting on a stool at the refreshment stand, nursing his badly bruised elbow. How was I going to get him back to the motel? Where would we find a doctor?

Behind the counter—on which stood sweating bottles of orange Fanta—was an old man, one of tens of thousands of such Mexicans, face lined from too many hard days in the sun. Reaching to a shelf below him, he pulled up a jar of something viscous, green, and evil smelling. Motioning Tony to move closer, the Indian slopped this gummy substance on my brother's elbow and massaged it gently. Within seconds, Tony reported that a warm, healing electricity had entered his arm, swiftly reducing the pain. Within minutes, we were able to walk to the ferry—which had not left—and made it back to our room. By this time, Tony was perfectly comfortable.

For the rest of the trip we referred to this as "The Magic of La Roqueta."

But the real magic of the trip was in the relationship with Tony. Traveling with him had created a brotherhood that had not existed before. We were more equals, more comrades, more *family* than ever before.

This golden time would never happen again. From then on a divide would exist between us.

In the years to come, I would think back to this trip often. I would refer to the food, the weather, and the experiences I had shared with my brother. These were roseate memories, lovingly preserved.

Chapter Ten

Kit's wedding, 1962

I RETURNED FROM MEXICO to find that my "girlfriend" was taking off for Europe for a postgraduation tour of architectural sites.

It is not an exaggeration to say that this threw me into a panic. What would she *do* while she was away? Forage for a new man? Explore the depths of his romantic soul? My fantasies ran the gamut.

And what would *I* do? How would I get by without her?

This *abandonment* (for that was how I experienced it) was the worst I had ever felt. I was in a fit of coruscating grief. Why was she doing this to me? Why did everyone always abandon me? It was a neurotic despair unlike anything I had gone through.

Then, as letters from abroad came one by one, I began to consider the possibility that she had not forgotten me—only gone on a lovely vacation. We wrote back and forth, and in one letter I asked her to marry me. She didn't reply.

In fact, two months later, when she returned, she said nothing about marriage. I waited, afraid to ask, becoming more and more unsure of myself, more and more panicked.

She never did say no, but I took her silence for a turndown. She was abandoning me, and I went into a period of intense anxiety. For two weeks, I was afraid to go to work, or indeed to go anywhere. I shut down.

Little by little with my psychoanalyst's help, I worked on what had encouraged me to get tied up with this woman in the first place. Had I perhaps *sensed* that she would never commit to me? Had I sabotaged myself from the beginning? Was I—in the words of the psychology profession—in an endless cycle of the repetition compulsion: the need to live through what had traumatized me in the first place, hoping over and over again that I might reverse history?

The relationship was over, and I needed to find a way to move on, to find the "right girl." In July of 1961, the mother of a high school roommate suggested that I meet the daughter of one of her friends. Susan Ries was twenty years old, an English and philosophy major at UCLA. I phoned the number I had been given.

"Bob's Big Boy" was how the young woman on the other end answered. Now, Bob's Big Boy was a fast-food restaurant in Los Angeles. I quickly hung up. Clearly, I had dialed incorrectly. I tried again.

The same young female voice answered, but this time she said, "Hello?"

"Hi," I said, relieved, not even taking the time to realize that I'd experienced a practical joke. "My name is Kit Lukas . . ."

There was a slight laugh on the other end of the phone. "Kit!" she said. "That's the hokiest name I've ever heard."

Susan's sense of humor might be just what I needed to pop my bubble of despair. Certainly she felt that I spent too much of my time being oh-so-serious about love, life, sex. At times, true to form, I couldn't believe that she was the right woman for me. After all, if she loved *me*, how could she be good enough? After she began to reciprocate my affection, I began to find reasons to have a fight, to pull away. If she loved me, then this couldn't be what I wanted, because the person whom I had most loved had deserted me. If she didn't love me, then I wanted her passionately, because I had to conquer the loss of childhood.

I recognized this behavior in Tony (who dated ferociously but for years couldn't find the "right woman"). But it took months for me to see it clearly in my relationship with Susan.

Six months, to be precise. In January, I proposed. On July 1, 1962, we were to be married. Tony would be best man.

Susan and Tony took to each other immediately. She was not put off by his dark moods, simply sought—as with me—to lighten them with her irrepressible joshing. On Dad's arrival for the wedding, he, too, could not believe how beautiful and charming Susan was. The only naysayer was Missy, who, like a Wicked Witch of the East, arrived with a cane, a scowl, and demands for attention.

On the day before the wedding, rather than adhere to Susan's mother's schedule for yet one more hair appointment, she, Tony, and I went to the racetrack, where we bet on numerous losing horses but enjoyed ourselves tremendously. After the wedding, just before we drove off to San Diego for our brief honeymoon, Tony confided to me, "If you hadn't married Susan, *I* would have."

The big news at the wedding was that Tony had been hired by the *New York Times*. He would start on the general assignment desk but would then be prepped for foreign duty either in Asia or in Africa; if he was lucky—and skillful—he would be sent to one of those plum European positions that foreign correspondents aspire to.

I don't think the family could have been prouder. Tony had shown us all that he had the right stuff. I knew it was the culmination of one dream, and the beginning of another. The culmination, because just *getting* a job on the *Times* had been his goal for over a decade. The beginning, because I knew that Tony would now shift his sights upward: to a higher rung of the ladder. If past predicted present, he would begin to berate himself for not climbing faster, harder, still higher.

After four months at the *Times*, Tony wrote me that the newspaper was sending him to the Congo on December 1. They clearly knew what they had in hand. But, true to form, Tony wrote a peculiar if not quixotic note:

> *I'm of course very happy about the idea in the abstract. But in more concrete terms, I have no great desire to spend two years in Léopoldville. I was just beginning to enjoy New York.*

For years, he had been striving to achieve this status. The mother of all journalism—the *Times*—was sending him abroad. Now that he *had* this prized possession, he was dispirited, discounting the rewards of his expertise and hard labor. It was a sign of things to come: forever doubting that what he aspired to was what he really wanted.

He was right. What he really wanted, and what *I* really wanted, was proof that we had not been abandoned and rejected, that we could regain our previous, childhood state of grace.

Nevertheless, Tony's first foreign assignment was to Léopoldville. His fragile command of French now bolstered by an intensive course at Berlitz, he set off with great excitement to learn about Kasavubu, Adoula, Mobutu, Moise Tshombe, Patrice Lumumba, the Pygmies, and how King Leopold II and the Belgians had destroyed a nation. Endless civil wars, which continue to this day, would show him that the king's legacy was . . . *more* bloodshed.

I knew what it meant for Tony to be abroad. I wouldn't have liked it: it would have been neither exciting nor a "romantic" enterprise, nor one I would dream of taking on. But *he* wanted the job, and despite leaving safety and family behind, he would conquer the work and, on some level, feel gratified by it.

Once Tony got to the Congo, he stopped writing home almost entirely. Dad complained bitterly that he didn't hear from his elder son. To me, Tony sent only two letters during his two-year stay in the Congo, but each gave insight into the beginning career—as well as the inner emotions—of this foreign correspondent.

He *did* thank Susan and me for sending him paperbacks. He remarked that he particularly enjoyed Durrell's *Alexandria Quartet* and Mark Harris's *Southpaw*. Conrad, Malamud, and Waugh were also on his list.

And he reported on the dangers of following the civil war to its heart of darkness. Tony and fellow journalists Arnaud de Borchgrave and Jon Randal came under attack at one point. All the men in the town were herded into a small building by local government officials and a CIA operative, given a weird assortment of guns, and told to protect themselves if the rebels came close. Tony's army training may or may not have come in handy. He didn't say. He did say that even in the midst of battle, he remembered to take his antimalaria pills.

There was also a revealing story about how Tony's ever-present anger could boil over at any point.

Mobutu Sese Seko had taken over the country in a coup. He called a press conference. When Tony arrived at governmental headquarters, he found that soldiers were checking identification of all journalists. The ID package had been changed recently, but Tony had neglected to collect his new papers. The soldiers refused to admit him to the news conference. He struggled with them in his serviceable French, but to no avail. Furious that someone reporting for another newspaper might get hold of this important story, depleted from long service in a strife-torn country, bogged down in humidity, Tony reverted to curses. *"Je m'en fou de vous,"* he said, *"de vous et de Mobutu."* The translation runs something like: "Fuck you and the president you rode in on." Tony was marched off to jail, to await a *Times* lawyer to get him out. In retrospect, the story was told with a sense of humor and bravado. But *what*, as the narrator in *Peter and the Wolf* says, what if the soldier had used his rifle?

In Tony's next assignment, India—a step up in the journey to top foreign posts—life was a good deal better, and the letters flowed more often.

India provided him with high living: a house with three servants, plenty of room for entertaining, a patio with tropical birds, a car and driver. He traveled widely and came to respect the country and its people.

More important, his reporting made it to the front page during perilous times in that country. The Pakistan-India wars were heating up over Kashmir. There were threats of building nuclear deterrents on both sides. And Russia was making noises from the north. Tony had long ago earned his stars, and the *Times* brass thought highly of him.

THE NEW YORK TIMES
I. E. N. S. BUILDING, RAFI MARG, NEW DELHI
J. ANTHONY LUKAS, CHIEF OF BUREAU

August 25th, 1965—
This is an ideal country for the kind of writing I like to do—the sort of slightly offbeat, bizarre feature story which nevertheless has plenty of political, social, economic, linguistic, philosophical, and psychiatric overtones (look for them next time you read one). The bottom drawer of my desk is just filled with

lovely ideas for such stories and more go in every day. I've de-
cided that I like India as a field for journalistic endeavor.
I don't like it at all as a field for just about anything else. Like
women. Like, there aren't any. After my two and a half months
of philandering in New York [on leave], the past four months of
celibacy have been hard to take. I've been working hard, but I'm
one of those guys who can't forget the other things life has to offer.

He did play tennis, go to the movies, go on dates, but it was clear
that none of this was enough to satisfy his need for companionship.

He gave over more and more of his thinking to his status as a
single man and why he couldn't find the "right woman." Still,
while he might worry about his personal life, it was always the
professional one that he came back to—on paper and in practice.
He wondered if he wouldn't be better off quitting the *Times* and
going freelance. He'd lose money and prestige, perhaps, but get to
do "a really solid piece of work." What was insubstantial about
the work he'd done for the *Times* was unclear.

Perhaps it was not solidity of work that was the problem so
much as the old depressive devil. While he had now found a female companion, who moved in with him, he spoke more often of
his pain when she went away than he did of the pleasure of having her there. He once wrote that his "gazelle" had gone to Bombay to look after her ill mother. "I'm melancholy."

To Dad he found it necessary to be more upbeat about life and
about his companion in particular. "She's a real delight—one of
the most vivacious and lively people I've ever known. Delhi seems
the grimmer for her absence. I may even take a jaunt down there
myself in the next few days so if you start seeing bylines from
Bombay you'll know what I'm up to."

Indeed, some Bombay bylines did show up, but Tony soon returned to home base in Delhi: plowing on, writing a huge piece on right-wing Hindu groups for the *New York Times Magazine*, traveling up and down the country, and proving his worth. In September 1966, he visited with Dad on the island of Menorca, off Spain. It was such an uncharacteristic place for either of them to have gone that the vacation was surreal. I think it was the first time that Tony came face-to-face with Dad's alcoholism.

> *The days in sunny Menorca were a little strained. Dad and I sat around the lobby and the bar of the Agamemnon drinking dry martinis and making rather desultory conversation. Nothing very significant was said by either party, but I think Dad got a lift out of it. I thought he looked a little better and more relaxed than when I saw him last, but he did some damn heavy drinking a couple of the days—you know the drill, nipping away at the bourbon bottle all afternoon and then starting on the martinis at night.*

His words left me puzzled and a little dizzy. I didn't know Dad had traveled outside the country, not since a few months he'd spent in Germany in the 1950s. I thought he was sedentary and U.S.-bound. It made me wonder where *else* he had secreted himself off to, without telling me. The idea of Tony and Dad going to tiny Menorca in the Mediterranean, a place known in those days mostly for stoned expatriates, was bewildering. I can imagine the scene—in a bar on some backstreet—and it isn't pretty.

In those days of blissful ignorance I didn't put Dad's drinking together with his moods. For me, and for everyone I knew, liquor was a treat, something you occasionally took to make you feel good. The idea that people were *dependent* on it—in those halcyon days before marijuana, crack, and other drugs of support hit the schoolyard markets—had not occurred to me. So the idea that Dad was an *alcoholic* and needed his drug never crossed my mind. He was someone who *liked* to drink, and he wanted to drink. The negative effects—his anger, his own depression—never hit home.

The worst instances of Dad's behavior due to drinking, the times I was most aware, were when Susan and I would be walking down the street with him and he would say, in a very loud voice, "Susan, you're a woman: explain that to me." "That" was a young woman nearby who had dyed hair or a low-cut blouse or some other fashion statement. Or "that" was an older woman with a fat belly. Or "that" was a young man with a hippy-dippy attitude or attire. Then the scorn that came over Dad was a far cry from the liberal father I had come to know.

At times like these—and they increased in number and amplitude over the last years of his life—I would look the other way, or cringe in embarrassment, or wish I could be somewhere, anywhere, but here. Later, Susan and I would laugh or cry over these episodes. But at the time, we said little. Alcoholism was not talked about among the general population. A man was either a drunk or a stone-cold-sober and upright person. Middle-class Jewish people didn't accept that their fathers could be drunks, so they must be upright citizens who occasionally took too much.

Like thousands of others, I deceived myself. I was an enabler, but I could not break free from my fears and anger, not nearly enough to help my father.

I wrote to Tony that Dad and Betty's marriage was now officially ended. Dad had waited until he could make sure that Betty got what was coming to her from her late husband's estate, while he eked out a living in a hotel room on Fifty-seventh Street. He had left behind all the belongings that he and my mother had acquired—antiques from France and Italy, and wedding gifts. He just wanted to get out of the apartment, he said, but I told Tony that I thought Dad had feelings of guilt over leaving and gave Betty all those beautiful belongings as atonement.

To Tony the divorce was inevitable, but something of a relief now that the angry marriage was over. He was also sad: "What kind of life is it for a man of sixty-five, living in a room and a half apartment in New York? Christ, I hope I don't end that way."

That was not a casual thought.

By the end of the year, Tony had decided not to extend his tour of duty for a third year, which the *Times* had offered him, and not to take a Belgrade post, which was an alternative. As for China? Learning the language was too much of a challenge for him. Barring appointment to the plums of Paris or Rome, he'd prefer to return to a place he could call home: New York City. He was in his early thirties.

I owe it to myself to give my Personal Life some attention after many years in which I have thought only about my career. It's high time I get married. Sooo—I've told the Times that I'd like to come home to New York for a year and work on the metropolitan staff. It will be just one year ... but if I can't find a wife in one year's hunting in New York then something is radically wrong. Naturally, I expect you and Susan to keep your eyes open for lissome young things these next seven months so that when I get back you can start parading them into my office for inspection.

Later. New Delhi. Tony is miserable:

I'm afraid things have not been going very well at this end for the past few months. I was bitterly unhappy at the Times' decision to put Joe Lelyveld in here eight months before my departure. Even

*though he is technically the second man in the bureau . . . this
seemed to me to be an unfortunate move.*

This reflects a perpetual issue for Tony, his "Halberstam
dilemma."

The fact that my brother never made managing editor at the
Crimson, and David did, bedeviled Tony for years. It began a lifelong rivalry with David, of which Halberstam himself was perhaps never aware. In Tony's view David was richer, more famous,
and more blessed than he. Halberstam got a job with the *New York
Times* before Tony. Halberstam got his first Pulitzer before Tony.
My brother's need to be "the best there is" never let him believe he
was successful *enough*. The disparity—or perceived disparity—
between David and himself rankled.

This lack of self-worth, the jealousy, the sourness of spirit,
could spur him on at times—make him push for greater goals,
more perfect stories—but it could also send him into the depths of
depression.

So with Lelyveld, the dilemma raises its head again. In fact, I
cannot remember a year going by when some real—or potential or
imagined—rivalry did *not* raise its head to bite him. He was—and
would remain—sensitive to the juggling of hierarchies and positions.

In his final letter from India, he restates this dilemma:

*I confess I am returning to New York with great trepidations
about my future on the Times. In the last eight months almost
everything in my relations with the paper has turned sour. However, things may look brighter on 42nd street than they do here.*

In fact, things *did* look brighter, and Tony never returned to the
foreign field, except for special assignments. He found the work on

the metropolitan desk, under Arthur Gelb, rewarding. Here, he could write about Harlem or City Hall or Newburgh with the same kind of attention to detail and color, and with the same insights, he had brought to his work in India and the Congo, *and* enjoy the friends and family he had missed abroad.

MY LIFE HAD ALSO TAKEN A SERIES OF TURNS. Due to a variety of conflicts with Bob Maxwell, I found myself, just before my wedding, with no job. I despaired that I'd ever be in a position to support Susan, who was starting her first year of graduate studies at UCLA.

But in January, in one two-week period, I received two offers. One was for a TV series just starting up at MGM. The other was to join New York's public television station, Channel 13, WNDT (later to be WNET).

We leaped at the opportunity to move to New York, to be closer to Tony when he came home on leave, my father, and the exciting theater there. Susan abandoned grad school.

Tony wrote from the Congo that he was delighted to hear that I'd moved from the "fleshpots of L.A." to the serious world of New York.

As I look back at the correspondence from Tony, the fact that there were fewer rather than more letters makes each one have a weight that it doesn't necessarily deserve. The same is true of my mother's letters to Dad. Sometimes—as Freud said in another context—a letter is just a letter, not a cry for help or a metaphor.

Nevertheless, because there were few, I awaited them eagerly and opened them quickly. These were the times that Tony let himself express positive and negative feelings openly, where he said what was on his mind. In person, he came across as a serious, guarded, often depressed, or angry character—deep, sad eyes with dark circles under them; low, lugubrious voice—but on paper he could allow his wishes and desires and disappointments to emanate.

As the years went on, it was also the only place that Tony now allowed himself to embrace me as a friend and brother. For instance, from the Congo came this, reacting to an Emmy I won:

A long overdue congratulations on your Emmy. You are becoming emmynenter and emmynenter by the day. I want you to know that I'm damned proud of you.

As I turned thirty, I was made director of cultural programming.

Well done, chappie, as they say "out here." [By now, he's in India.] I know how hard you've worked for this promotion and— although I've seen very little of what you've done—I'm told by Jack Gould that you're the hottest thing since Milton Berle. The title is very impressive indeed. Do you get a rug on the floor too? And a beautiful secretary? And six TV sets in different colors on which you can watch the major channels simultaneously? And a cringing yes man who shuffles into the office and says "great idea, CW," and "You're the hottest thing since Milton Berle, CW?" Seriously though, CW, heartiest congratulations and long may you wave.

When Tony decided to come in out of the cold, to decline that third year as correspondent in India, Susan and I offered him a bedroom in our apartment. We were planning to have children, but because none had yet arrived, we thought that having him with us would be good for all of us. He was touched by this, but opted instead for the Harvard Club until he could find an apartment for himself. I think he was genuinely embarrassed at the thought of "having" to share with us, but there were probably other motivations, including his desire to look for a long-term relationship with a woman.

IN THE YEARS THAT FOLLOWED, Tony pursued his bliss at the *Times*, moving ever upward, gaining the accolades he deserved, writing stories that advanced daily journalism. He didn't always please his co-workers or his editors. Sometimes he was moody, sometimes combative, sometimes just a loner.

Occasionally, he would telephone or ask me over to his apartment to read a paragraph or even a page of a new piece. In all the time this practice went on—both with me and with colleagues—Tony always read aloud. He didn't permit us to take the pages into our own hands. I don't know whether he didn't trust us to use our eyes or whether this was more a way of hearing it for himself. Or perhaps just some of the Lukas zest for theatricality.

He did that with me when he wrote a famous piece on the Greenwich, Connecticut, teenager Linda Fitzpatrick, a front-page story that won him his first Pulitzer Prize. It was the late 1960s, the height of the hippy generation's hold on America. In San Francisco, the Haight was thriving. In New York, it was Greenwich Village that held sway. Fitzpatrick was living a double life: being a "normal" adolescent at her parents' home in Connecticut during the week, but using drugs and sleeping with addicts and down-and-outers in Greenwich Village on weekends. She was murdered, and Tony was put on the story.

When I arrived at Tony's apartment one night, he was in the throes of wrapping up the piece for the *Times*. He had kept his work on the project very quiet, since many people at the paper, as well as Fitzpatrick's parents, had it in their heads that Tony was going to paint Linda as "clean," anything but the drug user that she had been portrayed as previously. It was not to be, and few people, outside of his editor, knew what he had uncovered, how big a story it would be. None knew the style in which it was written—filmically cutting back and forth between the two Greenwiches—or that it would be a journalistic triumph.

Tony asked me not to tell anyone anything about the revelations, but he wanted to read me some of it. With a totally straight face, he said, "This is going to win me the Pulitzer." I took his statement with a pinch of salt; it seemed egregiously optimistic and grandiose. Besides, I thought, who thinks of prizes when the work isn't even finished? Apparently, Tony did, and when the full investigative story ran on the front page two days later, I understood the power of what he had been doing, and how important it was to him that he kept his eyes on the prize.

Daily journalism never quite got that exciting again for him, but the work was always interesting, and his reputation grew.

AT CHANNEL 13, I was able to win Emmys, rise to become director of programming, and produce hundreds of programs. Despite a psychological distance between us, Tony and I were equally proud of each other. Nonetheless, his great successes were always tempered by his interior sense of failure, of fraudulence. So, too, Tony was constantly afraid that he would be "found out," that an editor was going to "kill" his piece, that it wasn't good enough. He would often doubt his own craft and experience. He would tell me that things were going badly, when in fact they were just coasting, or actually progressing.

I could see what Tony could not, that he was always a step ahead of everyone else in our crowd. He was intellectually advanced, well-read, and a superior writer and researcher. And he always believed that he could keep escalating his abilities, keep winning prizes, keep doing more—and better. He told one date that he hoped to win the Nobel Prize someday.

I, too, always felt I was not *good enough* at what I did. On some level—bizarre as it may sound—I believed that if I were as creative as I *should* have been, if I were truly a beautiful person, then Mother wouldn't have abandoned me!

While Tony and I were moving up our ladders, Dad was changing gears, too. In the 1960s, he became deeply involved in civil rights causes and organizations and went to the South to defend black men and women in courts where few white Southern attorneys wanted to go, and few black lawyers were allowed.

I had never been as brave, nor as able in public service, but I began to think of my work at Channel 13 as a way I could contribute to the world. In those days of the deepening civil rights and antiwar movements, I asked myself about each program: Does it advance equality among Americans? Does it give unpopular views a hearing? Do we hear enough about what is right, as well as what is wrong, with our world?

If Tony thought about his work in the same way, I never heard such sentiments expressed. Proud as he was of Dad's civil rights activities, as a journalist he believed his role was simply to write objectively about the world. On the other hand, as a private person, he contributed his time to the Committee to Protect Journalists and the Authors Guild; also, he helped young reporters on their way up. In fact, some have written that he was the preeminent "quiet" journalist in America: the reporter who was not in the limelight because he took such care (and time) to write his books, but whose efforts on behalf of younger talented writers and journalists were stellar.

In 1970, a new general manager came to Channel 13, which meant a management shake-up. In 1971 I was again out of a job.

I secured myself six months' severance pay. Susan, our two young daughters, and I went off to Aspen, Colorado, for the summer, to figure out the rest of our lives. It was a glorious summer, but I didn't have the slightest idea what my professional future would turn out to be.

About a month into the summer, Tony joined us for a vacation. He had already won the Pulitzer for his story on Linda Fitzpatrick and had published a book on disaffected youth, *Don't Shoot—We Are Your Children!* as well as his slim but famous book on the Chicago Eight conspiracy trial, *The Barnyard Epithet and Other Obscenities.* He was the Chicago bureau chief at the time of the trial and returned to New York after the book was published. He came to Colorado both for a well-earned vacation and to do some of what I was doing: figure out his future. It would not be long before he left the *Times* for good, choosing the freelancer's route.

One weekday afternoon, as the cumulus clouds drifted overhead, revealing occasional bursts of great sunshine, Tony, Susan, and I rented horses and some fishing gear and rode an hour up into the mountains to a pristine lake where, the locals said, beautiful trout awaited us. Tony had not ridden since Santa Fe; as Susan and I watched him, dressed in what we always thought of as his Harvard uniform—cordovan shoes, a wool pullover sweater, gray slacks—climb unsteadily atop the stocky horse the stable provided him ("Does he really know how to ride?" queried the wrangler), we leaped nimbly aboard our own steeds, but began to wonder if this was the best idea in the world. Nonetheless, with sandwiches, fresh worms, and light hearts, we took off for the lake, which was at eight thousand feet above sea level.

The horses knew their way, so we relaxed on the way up, joking back and forth about the fish we hoped to catch. At the top, as the crystal lake reflected a crystal sky, we let the horses graze and set to work to best each other at fishing.

Three hours later, neither nibble nor catch. Clouds began to cover the sky, darkening at the horizon; it was getting chilly. Clearly, a storm was coming, and neither Susan nor I wanted to remain at the lake without shelter. Tony, on the other hand, had come to the mountain to catch trout. He was unwilling to leave and begged us for another half hour so that he would not have to return to New York without word of his prowess. Reluctantly, Susan and I acquiesced. A few minutes later the first drops fell, increasing with frightening speed into a downpour. Thunder rumbled. We packed up.

As sure-footed as the animals had been on the way up, they were even better on the way down. We let them pick their path along the often tricky route. Soon, despite my rain jacket and hat, I was soaked. So was Susan. Tony, who had not brought a jacket or a hat, was dripping with cold water. His expensive wool sweater was soaked through, and I worried that it would shrink on him if we hit sunnier weather.

There was no jocular banter this time. It took us an hour and a half to wind our way down to the stable, where we all rushed to our little rental Toyota, undressed to our underwear, and drove home with the heater blasting.

Like many adventures, scary *during* the episode, our eventual safety provided all of us with a sense of derring-do in years to come. If we didn't exactly dine off this experience, we could remember it with pleasure.

Chapter Eleven

Kit, Megan, Edwin J., and Missy, 1968

IN OUR FAMILY, the old seemed to die with terrible reverberations of how the young had perished. Again and again their deaths were marked by depression, bipolar disorder, and suicidal disappointment.

Missy came first. In January of 1970, suffering from heart problems, she was moved to Philadelphia by Uncle Ira and settled in a nursing home. The day after she got there, she took an overdose of sleeping pills. A depressive for her entire life, she was never satisfied with the love she got from her children and grandchildren. She felt abandoned by me—when I married, and when I did not follow her to the Philadelphia hospital. She died, in 1971, at the age of eighty-seven.

Two years later, Dad died. At the age of seventy-one, his liver weakened by endless drinking, his body not up to the stress of all that abuse, he had a stroke. Susan and I had moved to England the year before, both to escape Richard Nixon's America and for me to look for exciting work.

While I was job hunting—and Susan and the kids were acclimating to the English pace—Tony phoned from Washington, where he was working on a huge piece on Watergate for the *New York Times Magazine*. It was time to say good-bye to our father, who had retired to California. We agreed that he and I would meet on the West Coast at the hospital.

When we arrived, it was not clear whether Dad would last a long time in his coma or would die soon. Tony and I talked about it over dinner near Dad's apartment in Tiburon. The doctors could give us little accurate information.

"I've got to get back to Washington," Tony said. "The *Times* needs this piece. It's going to take up the *whole* magazine; nothing else."

I understood. But I, too, had a conflict. Susan had just heard that her first book, *Fat Emily*, would be published. Her editor was coming to England to work on the final copy with her. I needed to take care of the girls while she did work on that.

Tony and I decided that we would both go back to our respective obligations, leaving Dad at the hospital; we'd return as soon as something "happened."

Within two weeks, Dad awoke from the coma and was sent to a nursing home. Tony visited him, then I replaced him at Dad's bedside; the *Times* wanted a second piece on Watergate.

Dad was moving in and out of sleep, heavily sedated, his right side badly paralyzed. There was an open sore on one arm. This was a new experience for me. Ever since I could remember, I had always been with an active father, one from whom I sought support and praise. That man now lay helpless and dazed from sedatives. The moment of separation was on me, and I didn't know what to do. How was I supposed to act?

He'd rubbed his paralyzed arm, turning and twisting to get comfortable, and it had become raw. They now had him restrained and sedated. As he slept, I sat by his bed quietly, which was characteristic of our relationship. My fear of his power and anger dampened any real give-and-take. He would awake for brief periods, look at me in surprise as if he didn't remember I was there, and then soon go back to sleep.

What I do remember him saying, shortly before I left that morning, was that he hoped Tony would find a woman to marry pretty soon. Shortly after he told me that wish, he complained of an ache in his left shoulder, and I massaged it until he fell asleep. In the years since, I have often thought of that moment as the one and only time that I actually gave him comfort.

Tony told me that he, too, had had a "last talk" with Dad. He mentioned nothing about "finding a bride," but said Dad hoped *I'd* find a job soon and "be happy."

Those dual wishes, told to the wrong sons, have always stood as a symbol of the miscommunication between us. Not that I thought Dad wished me ill, but a heartfelt statement of love would have been very welcome at that time—when I'd been drifting for so long. And he was leaving us.

Tony reported that Dad's last words to him of any kind were "Shit, piss, and corruption," and then he fell asleep.

That was more like him.

Before Dad's death, after we knew he was ill, Susan and I made plans to move to San Francisco, to be near him as long as he lived. Maybe I could jump-start my career back in the States. It was not going anywhere in London. Before we could even move, however, Tony phoned to say that Dad had died.

I didn't cry, not at that moment. It all seemed too futile, too far away emotionally. I thought, maybe I've done all my crying for dead people. Maybe I should reserve it for the living.

In my files, there is a letter from Ernst Kris, one of Freud's American disciples. It's handwritten on staid stationery, dated September 20, 1942. Dad had been in analysis with Kris, but only briefly. The tuberculosis would interrupt that work.

My dear Mr. Lukas:

It is with distress that I learned from your letter that what must be a period of agonizing inactivity has been superimposed upon the difficulties which of late have become your share. Naturally, no other consideration should now gain precedence over the wish to restore your physical health as fully as possible. After that, I feel certain, you will be able to re-assume with new vigor the new career, so successfully started in so short a time, to re-establish the home for your children—and I hope— "get yourself analyzed."

While not enough clarity exists about the interrelation of physical and mental states, it seems to me that the old doctrine of worries as contributing to disease is so amply confirmed by recent findings that your condition should at a later date re-inform your inclination to undergo the treatment interrupted last year.

Much luck for your recovery.

But Dad never did return to therapy. Tony's psychotherapy—recently ended—had lasted no longer than our father's.

In the midst of his second Watergate piece, Tony spent part of the early summer in San Francisco, clearing up Dad's meager belongings, and part in D.C., finishing the article. Then all of us joined up in New York for Dad's memorial service. It was held in a small room at the Society for Ethical Culture. The ashes went to a Hungarian burial society. That seemed fitting.

Ira and his wife, Frances, came up from Philadelphia to babysit the kids while we went to the service. Susan, Tony, and I sat together. As the moderately large crowd listened to the speakers extol Dad's virtues, Susan began to cry and took our hands. Both of us also wept. The service was attended by luminaries from the civil rights movement and reinforced my belief that Dad, despite his own despair at "not having accomplished anything" during his seventy-one years, was an important figure.

Tony later told me a final, sad story about Dad and Aunt Judy.

I don't know whether they made amends or not, whether they forgave what needed to be forgiven, but in any event she had replaced Tony at Dad's bedside, especially near the end of his life. One afternoon, after Dad had died, Judy sat at lunch with Tony and berated him for not spending enough time in California with our father. Stung by this accusation, Tony lost his cool.

"And where were *you* when he needed you all those years?" he snapped back.

She slapped his face and burst into tears.

Shortly thereafter, Aunt Frances was diagnosed with throat cancer. She had survived lung cancer some years earlier, but now this brave, thoughtful woman, who had paid loving attention to the needs of her brother-in-law (my father) and his sons, needed attention paid to her. But she was in such pain that we were cautioned not to expect much from a visit. Nevertheless, we went down to Jenkintown—Susan and I—and sat talking to my aunt for a few hours. Frances tried to carry on that conversation, but it was all too difficult. We cut our weekend visit short. After a painful year, she asked that an overdose of painkillers be administered by her physicians. They agreed, and she died of her own time and choosing. I considered this suicide an unwelcome addition to the family legacy, but I went to Jenkintown and spoke at her memorial service because I loved her and honored her. Strangely, despite the generally public acknowledgment of her "rational" assisted suicide, none of us at the service *spoke* of how she had died. I recognized my own hypocrisy in the matter. I had been the one to broadcast the "news" of Mother's suicide to my brother, and to others. Why was I silent here?

Only about a year later, Uncle Ira went into his bathroom and, in an anguished replication of his sister's death forty years earlier, cut his throat. His eldest son called us in New York with the news.

I was aghast. I did not believe history could repeat itself so directly. Tony said he wouldn't go. "I've had enough of suicide," he sputtered. I felt similar doubts, but again I went. Ira, too, had been a protector and a mentor to me, especially during my college years, when I would come over from Swarthmore to his house. He even set up blind dates for me. How could I *not* provide some solace at his service? Again, however, I said nothing of suicide in my talk. Again, I recognized my own hypocrisy.

If we had had enough of suicide, suicide was not through with us. In the 1980s, my ex-roommate Tom Russell, on his fiftieth birthday—recovering from alcoholism, but suffering from schizophrenia—took his own life.

I went into a deep depression. Though I didn't realize it, I was turning inward the anger I felt at all those people who were "abandoning" me or had done so in the past: mother, grandmother, aunt, uncle, best childhood friend, even my father, who had continued to drink in his isolated aerie in California, knowing it would kill him.

Why, Susan asked, did I drug myself with depression instead of feeling the anger?

"Read up on it," she said. "What it's like to be left behind after suicide. Maybe other people's experience can give you some help."

But there *were* no books on the subject. In the years before the words "physician-assisted suicide" had become popular parlance, or anyone had heard of Dr. Kevorkian, the silence surrounding the subject of suicide was pervasive.

A psychoanalyst friend, Henry Seiden, and I began to talk to *survivors* of suicide, those left behind. I discovered all sorts of companions—people who shared some of the feelings and conflicts that I had thought were only *my* fate. Susan helped make it clear to me: as I was doing, they were protecting others from their anger about these terrible acts, but not protecting themselves.

I didn't want *others* to undergo what I had experienced. And I didn't want to go through any more of the depression myself. Perhaps, paraphrasing the words of the satirist Tom Lehrer, I could do well for myself by doing good for others.

So Henry and I wrote *Silent Grief: Living in the Wake of Suicide*. It was about all the aftereffects: depression, anger, guilt, anxiety, replication of the act itself. We warned survivors that if they did not receive intervention in the form of comfort, therapy, and grief counseling, they, too, might end up as suicide statistics.

The book did, in fact, help me understand my own depression; my confusion over what I had experienced; my need for some way of saying good-bye to my mother—not simply ignoring that she had ever existed.

And it began to help others, too. I put a lot of energy into talking about the book on television and radio, spreading the word. Oprah and Donahue took me onto their airwaves. I was gratified when, among many who said I'd helped them, Bill Moyers wrote the following:

> I have waited a long time for this book. The secret grief that is at the soul of every survivor is in its own way a killer, slowly eroding one's ability to bear witness to life. The message of this book is redemptive: Life begins anew when silence ends. Lukas says the telling of this story helped him. Now, he has helped me.

In the early 1970s, Tony was beginning to feel the kind of depression that would become more and more severe. He had no permanent love relationships, no immediate prospect of a family of his own. Having won one Pulitzer Prize, he saw David Halberstam—

and others—win a second and go on to write best-selling books. The old jealousies were rising.

Some of this angst had already become apparent when we moved to England. After several months there, and after I had written Tony about our trip several times, and after my discovery that it would be hard to get work there, I was disappointed not to hear from him. We had even invited him to spend Christmas with us in London. Nothing. It would have been good to have him share the holiday with us. We missed him.

Finally I heard. Tony said that his pride had kept him from admitting to us—and to himself—how "wrenching" our move to England was for him. It had caused "an inexpressible loneliness and sense of loss." Susan and I had never seen him so emotionally expressive before.

> *Ultimately I realized the great guilt I felt about my dependence on you both—for discussion of the most intimate matters; for the warmth of a home to which I belonged even peripherally; for the love and understanding which I should long since have found elsewhere.*
>
> *I enjoyed our Sunday night dinners, our monopoly and chess games; most of all the Dictionary games in which I bested Sue. Being "Uncle Tony" to Megan and Gaby, having you both read and criticize my work, traveling to Philadelphia together for Christmases and other holidays.*

He should—he avows—have his own love, his own family, his own niche. He goes on to say that his "analysis" was helping in that regard. (In fact, it was a very short-lived psychotherapy. He would decide, after less than a year, that he was getting little from it.)

Finally, in a statement typical of the grief caused by long silences and the fantasies they create in our heads, he ends, "I'm writing now because I realized that to extend my silence any further would be to damage our relationship, perhaps irredeemably. I hope I haven't done so already, because I value it as I value few things in my life."

How much misunderstanding there is in silences! I would never have given up our relationship, no matter what happened, certainly not for his lack of letter writing. I felt his pain sharply.

WHILE WE LIVED IN SAN FRANCISCO, Tony came for visits occasionally. We had him for Christmas two or three times. The last time, in 1977, Susan sent us both off to Reno to enjoy ourselves at the gaming tables. She bought the airplane tickets, reserved a hotel room, and gave us a little bit of cash. We lost our money in a few hours at the tables and slot machines, but enjoyed being with each other. After leaving the casinos, we traipsed through the town—a poor man's version of Vegas—peering into gun shops, taking in a bad movie and a travesty of a stage show, and talking about our lives.

A foggy, socked-in airport forced us to take a bus back home. We slept a lot, but we also talked about other rides we had been on together, including with Dad out west, and in Mexico. I enjoyed myself tremendously. It had been almost twenty years since we had spent that much time "alone together."

From San Diego, where he had gone to do a bit of research, Tony wrote a short note that ended: "I love all of you very much and I love being with you."

I believe Tony meant that. I believe that he enjoyed being connected to us and seeing what joy our family engendered. In the early days Tony was comfortable enough with our children. When he and Megan first met (she was two weeks old), she spit up on his best jacket, but he laughed it off. For baby Gabriela, he played "the ape," leaping around and making monkey noises. She loved it.

As our daughters entered their preteen years, however, Tony didn't know what to do with them. There was talk of going to Yankee games and of other activities, but we realized soon enough that Tony wasn't going to become a father, and he wasn't much suited to being an uncle, either.

Then, after we had settled again back East, a hard split came between us. It probably started earlier, when Susan and I were still in the process of moving to what she called "a beached whale of a house" in suburban New York on the west bank of the Hudson. The house was long and narrow and had thick stucco walls and lots of rooms, probably too many for the four of us. Still, high on a hill, it viewed the river and the Tappan Zee Bridge, and on spring afternoons we could see Pete Seeger's *Clearwater* sloop sail by. How could we not buy it? But we had yet to get an approval from the bank for our mortgage. Because I had no job, getting a mortgage would be a particular challenge. I needed help.

I AM STANDING on the sandy verge of a one-lane road on the New Jersey coast. This spit of land running north to south was where Uncle Ira and Aunt Frances occasionally went to seek peace and quiet. Frances was already suffering from the cancer that would kill her. Ira was aware that he would soon lose his wife. I had flown here with our two daughters because Susan and I felt that the cross-country trip by car was too arduous for them. She and her niece were driving some of our household goods in our old Volvo across the States. Also at Ira's were his younger son, his wife, and a small child of theirs. It was a crowded, steamy summer scene, and I was already feeling nervous and out of sorts when I went for my evening phone call from Susan.

Ira and Frances had no telephone in their rented house, so I had arranged to receive calls from Susan at a pay booth on a deserted street at nine each night, not far from the beach and the house.

That particular night, Susan called with a sense of urgency and anxiety. The bank had refused to give us the mortgage because I had no new job. She was sitting in a motel in Nebraska, midway to New York. I was stuck with the kids on the Jersey Shore. We talked for a few minutes as she told me the situation. My anxiety level rose second by second. No job. No money. No mortgage. No house.

I put in a call to Tony. He was single at the time. He had saved lots of money from his *Times* salary. I was sure he would help me out.

I told him that I was standing in a phone booth on the Jersey Shore, with moths flying around my head beneath the streetlight; I told him that I didn't know how to secure our mortgage without his help. I told him I was frightened.

"I don't understand," Tony said. "Why won't they give you the mortgage?"

Tony had no experience with loans on houses—or on anything else. He was a novice where banks were concerned. As patiently as I could, I explained the situation.

"They need a co-signer, Tony. Someone with an income above $50,000 a year." The bank was asking for someone to vouch for us, to back us up if there should be financial problems. I didn't expect any. I told Tony this.

There was a long pause. It was the kind of pause that had an inevitable outcome. Tony was preparing to say no. I had heard that no before.

He started out with a different tactic, however.

"I don't know that I have that kind of money."

"What do you mean?" I asked. It was my turn to be non-plussed.

"I don't think I made that much last year. Let me go check."

I could hear Tony riffling through some papers, but I already knew the answer. He came back on the line.

"Christopher," he said, using the formal moniker he some-times employed as a joke, but this time the voice was troubled and I knew he was miffed. "No, I didn't make $50,000 last year."

"Jesus, Tony, what am I going to do?"

Long pause.

"Well, why didn't you think of this before you chose the house?"

Eventually, Susan's brother co-signed, we got the house, and we always paid the monthly mortgage on our own.

But that night, standing in limbo, I felt terribly betrayed and lost. Whatever the reasons that Tony could not or would not help out at this time, I felt bitter about it. My big brother was not there for me. Just as he hadn't been there for me when I went off to school in 1942. When I really *needed* him.

IN THE LATE 1970S, Tony was working on *Common Ground*. It had taken him seven years to complete this epic book that interweaves the busing crisis in Boston with two key families: the (white) Mc-Goffs and the (black) Twymons. A third family, the Divers, was not directly involved in busing, but provided a kind of Greek cho-rus on the scene.

When it was announced that the book was coming out, I was eager to read it. As with all his work, he had taken the opportunity many times to call and read passages over the telephone. I knew enough not to make any suggestions about these testings: they were meant not for us but for him to hear the words out loud and to get positive feedback. I had liked what he told me about the book, liked what I'd heard.

When I actually read the book, I was disappointed. It didn't leap off the pages at me as it had when Tony read parts of it aloud. There was more detail and what I considered extraneous material than I preferred. I felt the book wasn't a slam dunk.

Clearly, I was wrong. The book got rave reviews and a Pulitzer Prize and was made into a television series. That should probably have made me reconsider my views.

It didn't, though I never told Tony I didn't like the book. When we were invited to the publication party, thrown at a luxurious East Side apartment, we went. There were dozens of literary luminaries, but no one that Susan and I knew. After a while, feeling ignored—and that we had paid our respects—we left.

It took a year before I learned how angry Tony was. I had called him many times in the interim, but we hadn't seen each other. And he had never called me—until now.

The phone call went something like this: "Christopher"—the voice as sonorous and serious as ever—"I haven't been in touch for a while because I couldn't believe what you and Susan did at the party for *Common Ground*. I have to tell you that I was very upset for a long time. But our relationship means too much to me to let this go on. I'd like to get together to talk about this."

We met for a drink, and Tony expressed to me his vast disappointment about our reaction to the party and the fact I'd never said whether I liked the book or not (though he had probably gathered how I felt). Again, I recognized Tony's intense need for total approval, love, and gratitude.

Still, in retrospect, I knew that we should have stuck it out at the party. Boredom should not have kept me from doing the right thing.

There is more to it than that. I now realize that Tony was to me what Halberstam was to him. I was jealous. Like Tony, I just couldn't accept that I had my own aptitudes, my own acclaim. I was married to a warm, loving, and talented woman. I had two loving and beloved children who would make anyone proud. Scribner's was about to publish *Silent Grief.*

But I retained jealousy and anger toward Tony. Why didn't some of his success rub off on me? Why, in fact, didn't he play big brother by putting me in touch with people who could give me a quicker, bigger leap up the ladder of success?

Because this didn't happen, I concluded that Tony had no faith in me.

The deep core of both our jealousies (mine of him, his of other writers, such as Halberstam) went back to childhood. As with many siblings, there was bound to be rivalry. I felt that Dad favored him over me, while he was sure that Dad did nothing but criticize him. If asked, I might easily have said, "Dad loves you more," and he might have said the same. This common, though unnerving, set of emotions usually gets ironed out as children grow into adults. My two grown daughters, with adulthood, have become close, confiding friends.

When traumas occur, however, no one makes the effort to sort out the conflicts, the negative feelings, the jealousies, the suspicions. In our case, neither of us raised these issues with the other. I, like Tony, continued to suspect that I had been the "outsider." Neither of us was able to look at relationships and family dynamics closely or correctly, or even honestly.

Tony felt competition more vividly, more dangerously than I. While I eventually took these matters up with psychoanalysts, Tony took them up with no one.

As Tony's depression deepened, there never seemed to be a way for us to examine the rift between us, or to heal it.

Chapter Twelve

White Plains, 1939

"WHY ARE YOU SO OBSESSED WITH DEATH?" Tony asked me one day out at Sag Harbor as we walked across the excruciatingly hot sand on the way to a refreshment stand. In 1982, at the age of forty-nine, Tony had wed Linda Healey, an editor at an important New York publishing firm, and they had bought a house on the eastern tip of Long Island. That weekend Susan and I joined them. He was referring to the kinds of television programs I was making about end-of-life care, and the books I was writing.

"I'm not," I retorted. "I'm obsessed with living."

He didn't get it, which was surprising, because he *had* understood why I wrote *Silent Grief*. On that occasion he had sent me the most moving communication I would ever receive from him and given me a publication party at his home, for both of which I was extremely grateful.

> *Dear Kit:*
>
> *An hour ago, I read the last page of Silent Grief. I sat for that time, with tears tickling the corners of my eyes, thinking back over 54 years of life . . .*
>
> *Your lucid—and eloquent—prose has stirred in me feelings which I've long repressed. As you know, I do constant battle against silent grief, sometimes succumbing to it as I did last year, sometimes holding it at bay with an arsenal of defenses I've assembled over the years. I've fled from the pain of our youths—*

and the melancholy which it has bred in me—by funneling all my energies into the written page, often at great cost to the rest of me . . . Now, the authenticity of your experience, and your determination to grapple with it openly, has brought us this brave and moving book. You have done what all true artists do with the pain of living—transformed it into something purging and redemptive. You have worked through your pain in such a way that it will allow others to see their lives more clearly and honestly.

You have helped me too, Christopher, through your love and loyalty over the years, through the generous warmth of your response to my crisis last year, and now with the bravery of this response to your own grief. I salute the courage of this book, I respect the skill of its execution, and I love the man who could write it.

The reference to "last year" was to that point in time when Tony was in desperate emotional straits. Having finished *Common Ground*, he was searching for something else to write. In the meantime, he wrote magazine articles as a freelancer, one of which had been syndicated nationally. Unfortunately, the article resulted in a libel suit. With no future income in sight, and with his reputation on the line, Tony went into a series of anxious and depressive fits that threatened to undo him entirely. On the phone, his voice was deep, slow, devoid of any life. Susan and I worried about him constantly.

One evening after work, I suggested we have dinner. We went to an Afghan restaurant on Manhattan's West Side. This was a modest place, with the cookstove in the front of a narrow storefront space. It specialized in spicy meat broiled on skewers. Tony and I had always relished this kind of exotic but simple place. That evening, however, Tony could not enjoy his meal. He told me how badly the suit was going; that the lawyers were botching the job; that he wasn't going to do what they told him to—he knew better. Just before dessert, he stood and said, "I have to get out of here!" His anxiety had reached such a level that he couldn't stay cooped up in this claustrophobic space. He went out to the sidewalk to wait for me. I paid, and we took a cab uptown.

By now, Susan had begun practicing as a psychotherapist and social worker. I asked her what we could do for Tony. She said his anxiety was probably an agitated depression, in which feelings of anxiety and irritability, even some *mania*, may predominate, rather than the lethargy and other kinds of symptoms we associate with a depressed person. A good psychiatrist and medication were called for.

When I visited with Tony again, his anxiety had lessened, but he seemed overwhelmingly sad and down. I asked him if he thought he might harm himself. When the answer was not immediately forthcoming—we were crossing Broadway at the time—I said that I would take him to a hospital right then if he couldn't assure me that he wasn't going to try to kill himself. He said he wouldn't. I took leave of him with some reservations. He prevailed in the lawsuit, but I kept at him to seek help for his depression. He did go to a psychiatrist and started taking antidepressants. Soon afterward, he signed a two-book contract with Simon & Schuster for a substantial advance. His mental health markedly improved.

I felt relieved and gratified that I had been able to help him. Tony's gratitude to me for seeing him through that particularly upsetting and dangerous episode was a sign of our love and his apparent well-being.

I hoped that things would go well for Tony, but he found it difficult to settle on a topic for either of the two books. He came up with many ideas and then discarded them. He worried that he would never find a subject that would allow him to follow *Common Ground* with another big hit. He felt he needed yet *another* Pulitzer, another best seller to make him feel alive.

ON RETURNING FROM MY FORTIETH REUNION AT PUTNEY IN 1992, at the age of fifty-seven, I too faced a challenge: I was diagnosed with lymphoma.

After twenty-two days of radiation, the doctors pronounced me in remission. I was painfully aware that Tony had not come to the hospital, or volunteered to do so during any of my treatment. Perhaps now his fear of illness, blood, and death applied not only to himself but to others. Or perhaps fear of one more loss in his life kept him away, but I fervently wished that he had spent more time on the phone with me—reassuring me, offering and giving love and support. I came to see the absence of his support as one more piece of evidence that our relationship had changed permanently. We were no longer brothers in arms—more brothers at arm's length. I wondered why my "loyalty" did not seem to be matched by his.

Tony's moods were increasingly volatile. Meanwhile, he had discovered a story that fascinated him: a town in Idaho and the murder of a governor named Steunenberg. The book would be called *Big Trouble*. He researched a long time and began writing, but found the book a struggle. It didn't have a neat ending, and that bothered him. If he wanted to be true to himself, he felt he should abandon the project. Linda tried to reassure him, as did I. He had had doubts before. Wasn't this just another depressive episode? He asserted it wasn't. Visits to his editor got him going again. It looked as if he'd finish the book within a year or so, and it was now going well.

By the mid-1990s I was again out of work. Tony was support-
ive. I remember him saying, "Hey, you shouldn't be depressed;
that's *my* act." Then, to my great surprise, he offered me financial
support. "Listen," he said, leaning forward in that earnest way I
had come to know over sixty-two years. "I've got plenty—well, I
don't mean *plenty plenty*—but I've got enough for the two of
us"—indicating himself and me—"so don't worry. If you need
any money, just ask me."

I marveled at these words. Whatever else Tony and I had been
to each other, we had not been financial safety nets. I was moved:
now, at last, my big brother was going to take care of me. I never
did need to take Tony up on his offer, but I felt his warm hand on
my back, holding me up at a time when I really needed it.

Looking back, I think it should have occurred to me that his
concern about the artistic success of *Big Trouble* and his cheerful
offer to help me financially were signs of something badly askew.
Cheerfulness in a depressed person can be a sign of bad things to
come, of the decision to end it all. With the decision made, depression miraculously lifts. I didn't pick up on the possibility.

In mid-May 1997, Megan, Linda, Susan, Tony, and I went to
see Ibsen's *A Doll's House* in a stunning production. Tony bought
the tickets and took us all to dinner. Gabriela was studying around
the clock for the bar exam and couldn't join us. After the play, the
women walked behind us as Tony and I talked about how much we
enjoyed the play, how many times we had seen plays together, and
how important drama had been to our lives.

I felt a difference in our relationship. This was a Tony who
seemed very pleased to be with me and my family. This was a
Tony who was finished with a big book and showed none of the
anxiety that he had exhibited only a few months earlier—that the
book wasn't good enough. This was a Tony more relaxed than I

had seen him in years. Again, in retrospect, I should have worried. But I didn't. I was too happy to be with him, to see him enjoying himself, to go to brilliant theater, and to talk about it with him.

Three weeks later, we returned home from a party and to the phone message from Linda.

Chapter Thirteen

The days dwindle down

THE ELEVATOR RISES much too slowly to the tenth floor. I don't recognize the man running it. Perhaps he's just a night-shift replacement. When we told him what floor we wanted, he mumbled something that sounded like commiseration. I thanked him, but he looked surprised. Perhaps I misunderstood. Maybe he just wanted to say hello.

The first thing that occurs when a person gets fatal news is emotional shock, blocking out the catastrophic events and feelings. Unlike physical injury, when the body goes into potentially lethal conditions, emotional shock can cause a peculiarly clear and uncluttered state of affairs. Numbness and a *lack* of elevated feelings can result. The mind may not be able to operate cleverly and quickly, but often the tears and grief and physical trembling that we think of as hallmarks of bad news wait their turn. So it is with me. As the elevator rises, I go back and forth between past and present. Even at this moment, today, as I write this, time fluctuates. Sometimes I am there, sometimes in the here and now.

Susan, standing close beside me, touching my flank, seems calm, but I wonder what turmoil is going on inside her head. Is she also in shock or, as often happens when crises come, simply thinking long and hard before reacting? Is she wondering how to approach Linda? How long it will be before I start crying or shouting? What to do if I go berserk? On the way in from the country, she asked me several times if I was okay, but how do you answer such a question under such circumstances? Still, I knew how I was *going* to feel: anger, physical pain, guilt, frustration; needing both retaliation and succor. And, possibly, the desire to kill myself, too.

I had taken this elevator ride many times over the past twelve years. Sometimes alone, often with Susan. It is my brother's building. It is 10A, my brother's apartment, that we were seeking. Normally, when we arrived, he would open the door quickly, combing his fingers through his black tousled hair—for which I envy him, mine having gone gray and missing years ago. His lopsided smile, paired with oversize lips, would greet us.

Normally, too, Steunenberg would bark. Tony named the little terrier after the governor who was the subject of *Big Trouble*. I can now hear Steunenberg's little feet join Linda's on the other side of the door, but like his master, he is quiet tonight. I am dreading this. (Linda was dreading it, too. Over the phone, she said to Susan, "Are you sure Kit wants to come? Can he do this?")

Inside, there are four people, friends of Tony's and Linda's, people I may have met before, though tonight I cannot accurately place anyone. I notice a fifth person: a young policeman stands nervously by the bedroom door, which is shut. He turns quickly away when I look at him. Everything is in pieces. Is my brother still here? Is he in that bedroom, lying on the bed? Has the medical examiner been here? Will there be questions for us? For me?

This apartment has never appealed to me, tonight less than ever, though I can see they have done attractive things with the living room since we were last here. There are long bookshelves down each side, painted a bright red, and the couches have new covers. The large coffee table has a bottle of vodka on it, almost empty. There are glasses, too. Susan and I decline.

Linda and I go off to a corner of the room, away from the others. We sit on a small sofa.

"What happened?" I ask. Of course, I *know* what happened, but not the details. And I do need to know everything. Linda seems eager to tell me.

"He went off to Idaho with that woman from the *Boston Globe*. They were doing a story—Simon & Schuster wanted it for publicity for *Big Trouble*. When he got there, he became depressed and didn't want to do any interviews. He didn't want to talk to anyone. So they came back."

I had last seen my brother three weeks earlier, when we all went to the theater. Before that, when the book was just about to go to press, his editor had asked for a few additional cuts. The final draft had been very long, but Tony didn't want to make the changes. His whole life, he had never wanted to make *other* people's cuts, no matter what he was writing: a book, an article, a magazine piece. No matter how long the piece was, it was *his*, and he wanted to keep decisions about it to himself. In this case, Linda said, he'd made some cuts to make everyone happy.

"And . . ." I prompted.

"He was terribly depressed," Linda said. "I thought he'd get over it like he always had. But this time history failed me. When he came back from the psychiatrist yesterday, it was worse."

For some years, Tony had been taking antidepressants, originally at my suggestion. His depression never disappeared, but it was markedly lessened. He was pleased with the psychopharmacologist. We had all been relieved by that.

Linda was still talking. What was she saying?

"I'm sorry, I didn't hear you," I said.

"I said she was surprised. At his depression. She wondered if *she* had done anything wrong."

"Who?" I asked.

Linda looked at me strangely.

"The *Boston Globe* writer," she said.

"But what about the medicine?"

"He was supposed to increase it. But he didn't. Or if he did, it didn't work fast enough. I called him from work several times today. We were going to meet at a party. I went, but he didn't show up. I got worried. Came home. About seven o'clock. And when I came in . . ." She stopped, gesturing to the other room.

We went back to the uncomfortable group around the coffee table, where Susan was trying to stay in the conversation. It was, at best, desultory. The phone rang, reminding me that we had to call our daughters. We had to let them know. One of the others came out of the kitchen. "It's the *New York Times*," he said. "They want to talk to you." He meant Linda.

When Linda went into the kitchen to take the phone, I learned that she had already called the *Times* to tell them that Tony was dead. I had a question I had to ask, but I didn't want to do it just yet, so we talked about how the others had learned about the event . . . biding time. The people began to look more and more familiar. Yes, of course, I had met them all before. One was a protégé of Tony's.

Linda came back.

"Do they know it's a suicide?" I asked.

"No," she said.

"I think that's a mistake," I said.

This is a big thing for me. Given my family's history with suicide, I always want suicide out in the open.

Linda was angry. "Tony was an accomplished artist, a writer. I don't want people to remember him for *this*!"

"But they'll find out," I said. "Then they'll think it's been held back from them. They'll think . . ." I left it unfinished, because this was not the time for this argument. She was right, but I was also right.

I decided it was time to face my brother. "Will you go with me?" I asked Susan.

"I don't know if I can," she said.

"Let's do it," I pleaded. "Then we'll call the girls."

We approached the policeman. It was an unusual sight in this living room. Here, we were more accustomed to family gatherings or literary discussions. In fact, I had never had a uniformed cop in my home before, or in that of any relative. Police were for domestic violence or robberies. We'd been burgled twice when we first moved to New York, but they sent detectives—in plain clothes— and there was nothing sinister about them. They stayed but a few moments. We never got our stuff back.

This cop had apparently been told to stand guard here until the medical examiner came to probe into this suspicious death, suspicious only because all apparent suicides are questionable until verified. I wondered what his orders were. Could I even enter the room? Could I touch my brother?

As we came up to him, I saw how truly young and fresh this boy-man was. I'm used to the bulky cop on the beat, covered with badges and ribbons, laden down with truncheon, handcuffs, Mace, a Taser, an automatic. This youngster didn't have any of these, as far as I could see. Perhaps he left them in his pack somewhere, or a patrol car. Perhaps he was far less accustomed to violent ends than I. Maybe this was his first deathwatch. What was he to do with the body of a stranger that was only a few hours away from life, whose last moments had been a desperate pull of a bathrobe cord around his neck as he lay on his bed?

The cop moved slightly toward us, and I thought for a minute he was going to bar the way.

"It's his brother," Susan said, and we slid past into the bedroom.

In the dim light from the bedside lamp, I turned, cautiously, to look at my brother's body. Tony was lying on the bed fully dressed, only one leg slightly drooped off the side. The room was dark; but Tony's rooms were always dark and messy.

Time slowed down, and I felt, curiously, stereotypically, in a dreamlike state.

Someone has removed the cord from around my brother's neck; without it, he could easily be asleep, his large form carelessly slung across the bed. I am surprised how serene he looks, his umber brow no longer creased, his fat, turned-up lips relaxed across his teeth, features less troubled than I have ever seen them. Only the slight bluish tinge to his dark complexion gives the clue that he is not breathing. I want to touch him, to know that it is my lifeless brother, my companion for sixty-two years—though separated often by physical and emotional distances. Still—my brother. Without touching him, I can't be *sure* he is dead. But the cop is watching, Susan is at my elbow, and, like most of us, I fear what a dead body might feel like.

Reticent and embarrassed by the situation, I cannot bring myself to reach out my hand, to verify my brother's death. As a result, were it not for the fact that I have been sitting in the other room, talking to those people about this event, I would be tempted to shout at him, "Get up and stop kidding around." I wish he would—and put an end to the nightmare that is just beginning.

How strange, I think: no sign of a struggle; no sign of agony. For once, he looks at peace. Even while I register the fact that this is a cliché, I see that it's true; he looks okay. And still I can't bring myself to touch him. I go as close to the bed as I can, then stop and try to remember this image. For the future.

On the bedside table is a clock, its electric second hand moving peacefully around the dial. Time hasn't stood still, I think. Isn't that peculiar!

Well past midnight. I turn to Susan. "Come on, let's go call the kids."

In Linda's kitchen—what used to be *their* kitchen—I was able to reach Megan (our eldest, at twenty-nine) on the phone. Her first, intuitive reaction was not for her own pain but for mine.

"Oh, Dad," she said. "I'm so sorry." We arranged to meet her downstairs at her apartment.

As we said good-bye, I realized that no one in the living room was crying. I felt that was strange, but then I realized that I hadn't cried yet, either. Maybe I never would.

At two in the morning, when our pounding on her apartment door brought our youngest, Gabriela, twenty-seven, groggy and bewildered, to open it, her reaction, too, was generous and instinctive. Tears welled from her luminous eyes, but her words and hugs were for my sorrow. "Oh, Dad," she sobbed. "Not again. You don't deserve this."

THE MORNING AFTER TONY'S DEATH, we were awakened by a phone call at seven-thirty. A friend had read the *Times*, where Tony's obituary was prominent on the front page, and was calling to ask what had happened. Having had only a couple of hours of sleep, I was not terribly gracious. Also, I thought the newspaper had pretty well summed things up. Nevertheless, we chatted for a while, and then I thought the way to handle the calls from close friends was to invite them to dinner that evening.

"Are you sure you're up to that?" Susan asked.

"No," I said, "but there's only one way to find out."

I had long since become the cook in the family, not only because Susan's office hours often stretched late into the evening, but because I enjoyed being the giver of sustenance to our family. I loved eating, and I loved cooking. I relished the sit-down, the conversation, the satisfied sighs. I like mothering people.

So I invited some with whom I felt especially close. And our daughters, of course. Ten or twelve altogether.

I cooked a large pot of spaghetti with homemade sauce. A salad. Bread. Wine. The good stuff.

We talked mainly about what everyone was doing. But we also talked about Tony's death. And we talked about what people remembered about my brother.

Looking back now, I cannot remember feeling any pain that night. As is the case with many who have had to face death, the trauma didn't have its greatest impact on me at that particular point in time. As I sat with those friends, I was grateful that they had responded to my need; I thought how lucky I was to have people who understood both my brother and me. They didn't sit through dinner saying, "I can't believe it. What a tragic event." They'd all had some inkling of the pain in his life.

In the months to come, we would go through all the ifs and whys. For now, it was good food, good friends, good comfort.

It didn't take long before other reactions set in. As the past caught up to me, I became very silent. I listened to my voice on the answering machine and thought it was Tony's. Just a week after his death, I began to have sharp pains in my right hand. Soon, it became difficult to pick things up, to write, to eat properly. "I've lost my right arm," I said to Susan. Gently, she suggested that the words had symbolic meaning. The interpretation soon struck an emotional note with me. He had not been my right arm any more than I was his. But I wished that he had been, that we had been sidekicks, cronies—had spent more time together, looked out for each other in our later years.

He was the brother I had. But he was also the brother I never had. And the irony of *Silent Grief* was that I had been able to help others, but not Tony.

Who would be my big brother, now that he was gone? I hated him for leaving me behind like that.

There was release in the tears that followed those thoughts. My hand and arm began to return to their normal state of usefulness. But the memory of that pain endures.

Six months later, I had recovered much of my equilibrium. I no longer suddenly burst into tears at the strangest moments, nor did I exclaim angrily at the dry cleaner, the gas station attendant, or my wife.

PEOPLE ASK WHY MY BROTHER KILLED HIMSELF.

"Why would such a gifted journalist, whose works have won all the prizes in the world, do such a thing?"

"He had so many friends, why would he want to leave them?"

"But what about all he had to live for?"

In a short space of time, I had a drawerful of articles written by reporters pondering the death of one who, like them, made a living out of trying to sort out the truth, separating fact from conjecture. They were hell-bent on making sense out of this event.

When they phoned, I told them that they were going to fail. I told them that the problem with suicide is that it is a senseless event. There *is* no why.

But of course that's wrong. There are numerous whys, though it's almost impossible, or unlikely, that any single one of them is "the answer" that people want to hear.

But I, too, have been trying to make sense of that event. Trying to procure an *answer* that will absolve us all from guilt and grief.

At first, ignoring his lifelong depression, I wondered if he'd gotten some terrible disease and didn't want to tell anyone. Years before, perhaps after a one-night stand with a prostitute or an affair with a promiscuous woman, he told me that he thought he might have AIDS. Was that it? Unlikely.

Susan and I had noticed that his teeth were rotting, or seemed to be. Was there some horrible ailment that frightened him and presaged pain and disability? In order to satisfy myself, I phoned his physician, an old friend who had treated me for some years before I moved away from New York. The doctor assured me that Tony had no serious illness. And then he said a peculiar thing.

"I always made sure not to give him a prescription for sleeping pills."

I didn't reply, because I already knew where that was leading us.

Some people suggested that Tony killed himself because he had become convinced that *Big Trouble* was not good enough. I think he thought *Big Trouble* wasn't good enough because he was *already* depressed. It was bad timing—the end of a nine-year writing journey that put him at the bottom of the psychological heap.

Or perhaps he died because those Pulitzers and other awards couldn't bind up the gaps in his personal experience, in his genetic makeup, in the physiology and the psyches of our parents and grandparents. Who he was and, more important, who he wasn't just didn't fit the pattern he desperately wanted. And he finally gave out.

Or Tony died because he finally turned his rage in on himself. Just how intense his anger was is revealed in a story that he himself told me. In 1972, he was on assignment for the *New York Times* in San Francisco. Feeling the need for female companionship, he went to the Tenderloin district. Every city has one—a number of blocks where bars, gambling, and prostitution thrive. Tony would have known where to go.

He entered one positively dismal place where he was immediately accosted by a B-girl who sat down to drink with him. When he went to pay for the drinks, the bartender asked for $50. Tony told me he felt suckered and said he wouldn't pay. When the bartender threatened to call the police, a violent rage erupted inside Tony—one that he couldn't control.

Throwing the remains of his drink in the bartender's face, he said, "Go fuck yourself." The bartender reached for a baseball bat and swung it at Tony's head. He ducked, but the prostitute attacked him from behind, using her high-heeled shoe as a weapon.

Luckily for everyone, the woman realized that murder would be a far worse result than losing fifty bucks. They let Tony go. He told me later that it was the most frightening moment of his life, but there was also something about the telling of the tale that was sad: a sense of fury at women who led him down the garden path, offering love, or at least sex, and then betraying him.

Or Tony died because when he finished *Big Trouble* he had no next task. Most creative people—especially writers—have postpartum depression. The applause they expect and hope for hasn't come yet; and maybe it won't. The adrenaline of the writing period has ceased to flow because they are no longer writing. There is dead silence—dead!

Tony and I had performed for our mother on the window bench. The sun shone, and Mother was beaming. She applauded our efforts. But he had been abandoned by her twice: A short while after his birth, she tried to kill herself and disappeared from his newborn life for a few months. Then, seven years later, she did it again. He was then and forever permanently alone. I believe that Tony never gave up hoping that his efforts would waken Mother from her long sleep. He wanted to hear—and see—her applause, to experience her beaming face just once more.

I understand that wish. Every morning, for many years, I have awakened, thinking: "I'm ready to kill myself." Then, afraid of those words, I soften the language. I think, "My God, this could be the day," a mournful, fear-filled expression of trepidation, a caution to myself that something terrible could happen, ignoring the fact that the worst thing that could happen had already happened, many years before.

Occasionally, I will think these deadly thoughts when driving across a long bridge, one high enough to be a sure killer if I were to turn my wheel sharply. But mainly it is in the morning, dredged up from the murk of my dream-filled sleep.

For a while I thought these suicidal thoughts were left over from my brother's death: after he died, I didn't want to live. But that isn't what they were. They were throwbacks to my childhood. Through therapy, and through experience, I have learned that they are ancient mantras that come from the days right after my mother's death. It is a metaphor for my unwillingness to accept the fact that my parents abandoned me before I was ready to take on the world.

The despair that attacks a small child's sense of well-being under such circumstances causes wretched responses. "I'm ready to kill myself " is a way out of the terrifying thought "How will I live without her? Who will comfort and protect me?" Death may appear to be an answer to all of that.

What happened to me was not the worst thing that can happen to a young boy. I could have grown up with no parents or with parents who beat me, or with rats in my bed. Or bombed out in Palestine or Lebanon. I didn't. But there was that series of suicides and abandonments in my childhood. I have always felt lost and frightened that there was no one to keep me safe, and that I would be better off dead, away from all dangers. A terrified despair.

For years and years I couldn't be satisfied by *product*, by the films I made or the books I wrote, no matter how beautiful they were or how well received, because the audience I wanted to applaud and praise me was already dead, long ago. Did Tony also feel this desperation? Did he want to die because the one person whose applause and praise he yearned for was not available? We'll never know.

But we *do* know that my father, my brother, and I felt failure where there was none; that we discounted prizes almost as soon as we got them; that the Lukas human condition was to reach for the stars but never to acknowledge when we'd gotten to the moon.

What's remarkable is—despite the terrible depression—how *much* Tony accomplished during his life. He was a prodigious writer, an acclaimed journalist. A creative person.

And it was *still* not enough.

I am sure that I never answered the question of why Tony killed himself to the satisfaction of my interlocutors. It was almost impossible to do so.

There is a parallel question that I have been more successful in answering: why *I* have not killed myself.

Epilogue

I WROTE THIS BOOK in the hope of coming to an understanding of my relationship with Tony. I believed that I would come to forgive him for his suicide and for abandoning us. And I hoped that in the process I would come to terms with the internal pain that caused him to exclude me from much of his life.

But, more than a decade later, I see that the worlds we existed in were not only sadly flawed but quite separate universes: their almost parallel trajectories kept us on different flight paths. Our interior and exterior realities were more experientially disparate than I had imagined.

I cannot penetrate entirely his view of the world—his need for perpetual love, for a kind of applause that in the end he could not accept even when offered.

Perhaps—if there is such a thing as fate—we were not destined to be understood or to be understanding.

Still, two things pain me: Am I—*should* I have been—my brother's keeper? And, after all is said and done, should I be able to forgive him for killing himself?

In the end, I have decided no—on both counts.

We are capable of only so much: only so many responsibilities, so many burdens we can shoulder. We were brothers, but we did not cause, nor could we solve, each other's problems. Tony was born with the blue genes that were his downfall. He spent his life half in pain and half in creative explosions.

He did not kill himself to hurt me and the others who were his friends—though his way of going could not help but hurt. It is that final hurt that makes me unable to forgive him. I know that he did not choose to spurn me in his death any more than he chose to spurn me in his life. But I cannot let go of the fact that by leaving without saying good-bye, he left me, once more, all alone.

IN 2002, at the age of sixty-seven, I started what I hoped would be a second career. I left filmmaking behind and returned to the acting I had done as a child on that window seat in our big white house in White Plains. After some meandering through community theater in our local town, I studied with a teacher of Shakespearean drama, performed in a production of *The Brothers Karamazov* off-off-Broadway, and then, to my surprise, was offered a chance to play the lead in *Krapp's Last Tape*, Samuel Beckett's one-act, one-man play about solitude, memory, loss, and desire.

So it was that, one night in June 2006, I found myself on the stage of a huge theater in New York City, in front of a crowd of over six hundred people who had come to hear James Joyce's *Ulysses* read from noon to midnight but were treated in the middle of the evening to a half-hour performance of Beckett's play. Krapp is alone on the stage—just me and a tape recorder, on which I hear myself: words ostensibly recorded thirty years earlier. At the end of the play, the lights dimmed and I went offstage. Then the applause began. The crowd got to its feet. It was a standing ovation for an amateur actor, doing a part for which he was by no means prepared artistically, but whose character was apparently brought into vibrancy by real-world experience.

I wish I could tell you that the applause and cheers satisfied my craving. I wish I could say that the next morning I arose, satisfied with my life and with my creativity. Or that I no longer needed to hear the congratulations from the professional actors who were piling back onstage to read Joyce's words that evening.

It isn't so. Just as Tony's prizes and the thousands of plaudits for his work didn't fill up the hole in his soul, the applause faded away into the night, and I was still left wanting.

For I, too, have blue genes. I, too, have a voracious wish for "more."

The question then becomes: If Tony was only the latest in a long line of family members who killed themselves, will I be the next? My uncle waited until he was in his early seventies to kill himself. My grandmother did it in her eighties. I am in the out-box now.

Hard as it may be to believe, in my adult life I have not had a single day when I felt wholly well—physically or emotionally. Every night I wake with stomach pains. My cancer has returned three times, and we continue to fight it off with the most current treatments. There are days—too many of them—when I ponder whether I would prefer to be dead and famous rather than alive and "just another striver" in the world of arts and crafts. Had my brother shown me a way out of the pain of never quite achieving a grander status, or had he shown me what happens when you *do* achieve that status and it's not enough?

Still, with full confidence, I know that I will never go into a room at the end of a day and kill myself.

Too many deaths in my family, too many suicides.

I will not follow suit.

In my return to acting—not to the childhood scenes on the dining-room window seat, but to Shakespeare and Chekhov and Beckett—I am doing something that can sustain me.

For I am a perennial survivor. I don't mean that I have some fated victim's life, but I have managed to live in the shadow of my legacy of suicide through connectivity and family and psycho-therapy, among other blessings.

Beyond those, beyond rational structures and supports, and whatever skills of life I possess, my survival has had an element of luck. Good luck in finding the right way to *talk* about the past; luck in finding the right therapist to *listen*; luck in finding the wife who would help me fight my depressive episodes and suffer through them with me; luck in having two extraordinary daughters with whom to share the good times; luck in being *born* with a disposition different from others in my family; and luck in finding ways to use the experiences in my life to help myself—and others.

If our genes are more good than bad, if our DNA or traumas don't cripple our ability to learn as we get older, if nothing sticks us to the past despairs, we can survive; we can *thrive*.

So, despite the despair, luck and inborn temperament enable me to get out of bed in the morning and into *life*. I know that my morning mantra subsides once I get on with my day. I know that there are still things to do that make my life meaningful, and that I can protect and comfort myself.

I have learned how to throw the shoe at the wall, how to grieve, how to talk about the events in my life so that I shift the burden a little more each time there is a sudden death. I have learned not to fall prey to my own implosive, self-destructive impulses.

IN LOOKING AT THE YEARS SINCE TONY'S SUICIDE, I can see that the two whys? collide: why Tony succumbed to despair and died, and why I have not.

They collide, and then, like wavy lines on an oscilloscope, part again.

My mother, my father, my uncle, my aunts, my grandmothers, and my brother are all dead.

But I am alive.

Envoi

As this book was going to press I faced another sudden, unexpected loss: Susan—friend, wife, mother, aunt, and grandmother, novelist, playwright, painter, psychotherapist—exemplary in all arenas—died; too young, too vigorous, far too precious to all of us to disappear so precipitously from our lives. We don't know exactly what caused her death—some aberration of the heart—but it's not important: her evaporation from our lives is what matters. The loss is profound.

I truly meant what I said with the words that form the dedication to this book (written before her death): Susan saved my life in more ways than one. She supported my writing and filmmaking because she knew being creative was my road to *psychological* salvation, as her works and good works were hers. She knew that our love, our travels, and our children were our *emotional* salvation. And she knew that empathy and generosity were the greatest gifts to bestow: she felt deeply, and gave generously to all. Her ability to forgive—except when someone hurt a child—was astonishing and wonderful to behold. Our own children, Megan and Gabriela, found her an invaluable companion, filled with an unsmotherable sense of humor. Whenever tension threatened to dismantle us, or events got too heavy, Susan would crack a joke and then—even as outsiders looked askance—say, "This is too important to be serious." Susan did not get to read this book—wanting to wait until it was published. I grieve not so much because I won't receive her measured and accurate response to it, but because she will not see how important her role was: as gentle critic, supporter, lover, partner. We buried Susan where and how she would have wanted it. An eclectic funeral, with a Scottish bagpiper high on the hill and stupid jokes mixing with impassioned, grief-filled speeches at the graveside. To say she will be missed is a paltry statement of gratitude for our lives together. Her demise makes the other deaths and crises in my life seem wan and unimportant.

Acknowledgments

First off, thanks to Linda Healey for permission to publish excerpts from Tony's letters. Also, to the Schamberg family for permission to use a crucial letter from Ira.

Also high up on this list is Christine Tomasino, my agent, who had faith in me many years ago, continued to encourage, uphold, and support my work, and saw possibilities in this book when others did not. For mentorship, perseverance, good humor, and knowing the field of publishing, she deserves a medal of honor—if I can ever devise one.

In the family-and-friend category, aside from Susan, there are our daughters, Megan and Gabriela, who kept me sane. And Rafael Abramovitz—old friend, who told me to keep writing and let no one stop me.

Finally, Charlie Conrad, my editor, whose immediate excitement for *Blue Genes* energized me and led me to keep working on it after I believed I had finished. As a young editor in the old tradition, he has shepherded this book through the publishing world with verve and great support.

CHRISTOPHER LUKAS has worked as a writer,
producer, and director in public and commercial
television, and has won Emmy Awards for his
programs. He is the author and coauthor of five
books. Lukas lives near New York City, where he is
continuing to make films, write books, and work as a
film and stage actor.

ABOUT THE TYPE

This book is set in Fournier, a digitized version of
the original font cut that was part of the Monotype
Corporation historical typeface revivals in the 1920s.

Fournier was created by the typographer and
printing historian Stanley Morison (1889–1967) and
grew out of his admiration for the type cuts of Pierre
Simon Fournier (1712–1768).